100 Ways John Paul II
Changed the World

T0204816

FOREWORD BY PAUL KENGOR

100 WAYS JOHN PAUL II
CHANGED
— THE —
WORLD

PATRICK NOVECOSKY

Our Sunday Visitor
Huntington, Indiana

Our Sunday Visitor Publishing Division
Our Sunday Visitor, Inc.
200 Noll Plaza
Huntington, IN 46750
www.osv.com
1-800-348-2440

ISBN: 978-1-68192-655-1 (Inventory No. T2513)
1. RELIGION—Christianity—Saints & Sainthood. 2. RELIGION—Christianity—Catholic. 3. RELIGION—Christianity—History.

eISBN: 978-1-68192-656-8
LCCN: 2019956954

Cover and interior design: Lindsey Riesen
Cover art: Chuck Fishman / Contributor/ Getty Images

PRINTED IN THE UNITED STATES OF AMERICA

*Dedicated to the memory
of my father,
George Martin Novecosky
(1937–2016)*

Thank you for always believing in me.

Timeline of Pope Saint John Paul II

1920: Karol Józef Wojtyła is born May 18, baptized June 20 in Wadowice, Poland.

1929: His mother dies; he receives first Communion.

1932: His older brother dies.

1938: Moves to Kraków with his father; enters Jagiellonian University.

1941: His father dies.

1942: Enters secret seminary in Kraków.

1946: Ordained a priest November 1.

1954: Begins teaching philosophy at Catholic University of Lublin.

1958: Ordained auxiliary bishop of Kraków September 28.

1962: Goes to Rome for first session of Second Vatican Council.

1963: Attends Vatican II second session; named archbishop of Kraków December 30.

1964: Installed as archbishop of Kraków; attends council's third session.

1965: Attends final council session.

1967: Made cardinal June 28.

1978: Elected 264th pope October 16.

1979: Makes the first of his 104 trips abroad as pope.

1981: Shot in Saint Peter's Square May 13.

1983: Promulgates new Code of Canon Law.

1984: Establishes diplomatic relations with United States.

1987: Attends first international World Youth Day in Argentina.

1989: Credited as key figure in collapse of communism in Eastern Europe.

1990: Issues first uniform law code for Eastern Catholic Churches.

1992: Issues official *Catechism of the Catholic Church*.

1994: Named *Time* magazine's "Man of the Year."

1999: Unseals Holy Door in Saint Peter's to start the Great Jubilee of the year 2000.

2000: Presides at jubilee year events in Rome; makes historic visit to Holy Land.

2003: Marks twenty-fifth anniversary as pope.

2004: Opens Year of the Eucharist.

2005: Publishes *Memory and Identity*; dies April 2, the eve of Divine Mercy Sunday.

2011: Beatified by Pope Benedict XVI May 1.

2014: Canonized by Pope Francis April 27 (Divine Mercy Sunday).

Contents

Foreword

M any times over the years, watching and studying and writing about John Paul II, I asked myself, *how many ways has this man changed the world*? Evidently, Patrick Novecosky has asked himself the same question and had the smarts and skills to create a list. What he has produced is a unique list that I wouldn't have created, nor would anyone else. This is his list, eclectic and unconventional, with quite a few choices that will make people pause, raise eyebrows, but surely approve of and find illuminating and inspiring. There is truly something here for everyone, and truly many a notable thing that the late, great pope did to change the world.

I will not attempt to fully summarize the list here in this foreword, but a few things really struck me.

First, to begin this compilation with religious freedom is especially apt, given what John Paul II experienced so acutely in Poland as Karol Wojtyła, living under the jackboots of Nazi and Soviet repression. We in America and the West today face threats to our religious liberty as well. While they are nowhere near the same in terms of sheer violence, we nonetheless face threats like never before, and John Paul II would not be surprised. He feared that the West defeated Nazi and Soviet totalitarianism only to rush headlong into radical secular materialism and an unhinged moral relativism. That is where we are in the twenty-first century, and it is those forces that today harass, sue, fine, jail, dehumanize, and demonize Catholics and other Christians who refuse to applaud their attempted fundamental transformation of the culture and the human person. John Paul II told the United

Nations in 1995 that it must "safeguard the fundamental right to freedom of religion and freedom of conscience." These were the very "cornerstones" of human rights and a genuinely free society. "No one," he told the United Nations, "is permitted to suppress those rights by using coercive power to impose an answer to the mystery of man."

Every American living today should read those words, even if far too many refuse to listen. Beginning this list of 100 ways John Paul II changed the world with religious liberty is therefore fitting and essential. It signals the timeliness, if not timelessness, of this list, which tackles head-on hot-button issues ranging from Islam to homosexuality, abortion, and much more.

After starting with religious freedom, the list goes to the topic of dying with dignity, which is a wonderful choice by Patrick, before addressing subjects and individuals such as the Shroud of Turin, Padre Pio, Fulton Sheen, theatre, Fátima, surviving assassination, Ronald Reagan, Mother Teresa, Our Lady of Guadalupe, liberation theology, socialism, angels, the Jesuits, Galileo, Cuba, Italy, women, suffering, sex abuse, Medjugorje, Faustina, Joseph Ratzinger, marriage, the family, the unborn, the Splendor of Truth, the Eucharist, Mary, Vatican II, the Culture of Life, Divine Mercy, and finishing, appropriately, with the New Evangelization — which, in essence, is what this compilation by Patrick accomplishes. This book evangelizes in a new way by featuring the very words and works of the man who urged a New Evangelization.

To that end, Patrick quotes John Paul II from over three decades ago, in 1988, one of numerous occasions where in retrospect it seems like the man had a crystal ball: "[T]he present-day phenomenon of secularism is truly serious, not simply as regards the individual, but in some ways, as regards whole communities, as the [Second Vatican] Council has already indicated: 'Growing numbers of people are abandoning religion in practice.' At other times I myself have recalled the phenomenon of de-Christianization that strikes longstanding Christian people, and which continually calls for a re-evangelization.'"

We in the West are in the throes of a tragic, voluntary de-Christianization. People are wittingly abandoning religion in practice.

Even flagging all that I did here in this foreword is insufficient. Indeed, one of Patrick's categories is John Paul II's stunning level of productivity, which was extraordinary. The man produced a breathtaking theological legacy (another category), from numerous encyclicals and an updated *Catechism* and Rosary to approving a huge number of saints (still more categories). What this pope accomplished is stunning to behold, and not easy to capture, even with a list of a hundred examples.

There is something intriguing if not fascinating for everyone in this book. And though I started this foreword by saying that this isn't a list I would have devised, when Patrick asked me if I could think of anything he missed, well, I really couldn't. Here I've flagged not even half his examples — the ones that I immediately turned to after glimpsing the table of contents. I found myself taking notes as I went along. I've written two books on John Paul II, many articles, and have lectured and spoken on the man countless times, and yet there were things here that I learned for the first time.

As readers forge ahead with this book, they should do so confidently, learning and integrating the thoughts and exhortations of Pope Saint John Paul II. Many of these, from his teachings on the family to Divine Mercy to his Theology of the Body, constitute (as biographer George Weigel said of the Theology of the Body) "a kind of theological time bomb set to go off, with dramatic consequences, sometime in the third millennium of the Church."

I would hasten to add that this constitutes a theological time bomb not only for the Church but the world, especially a Western world awash in what John Paul II's successor described as a "dictatorship of relativism." Standing strong amid that dictatorship will take courage, and it will take an understanding of the teachings of this great pope.

Catholics and other Christians generally should take those lessons to heart and into their families and schools and culture. They should, to borrow from another category on Patrick's list, heed Pope John Paul II's timeless advice to *be not afraid.*

DR. PAUL KENGOR

Professor of political science and executive director of the Center for Vision & Values at Grove City College. Author of The Divine Plan: John Paul II, Ronald Reagan, and the Dramatic End of the Cold War.

Introduction

I've always been "lucky." When I was a teenager, local radio disc jockeys knew me because I always called in — and was usually the winning caller. It was only partially luck: after a few attempts, I developed a system that gave me an edge, even on our old rotary-dial phone. I learned early in life that you can, to an extent, make your own luck. As I got older and grew in my faith, I learned that luck really isn't luck. Everything — whether we perceive it as good or bad luck — is a blessing. As Saint Paul told the Romans, "We know that in everything God works for good with those who love him, who are called according to his purpose" (Rom 8:28).

That's why, when I won a raffle drawing for a trip to Cancun just before Christmas 1996, I knew God was up to something. At the time, I was a young journalist working for the Marians of the Immaculate Conception. I had no desire to sit on a beach in Mexico, but I had always dreamed of visiting Rome, so I called the travel agency that had donated the prize and asked if I could swap out the ticket. The travel agency agreed, and the Marians arranged for me to stay at their monastery in Rome with an ambitious agenda beyond the Eternal City. Pope John Paul II had asked the Marians to lead the re-evangelization of Eastern Europe. In the fall of 1997, my task was to travel to these countries, interview Marian priests who had been situated behind the Iron Curtain during communist rule, and tell their stories in *Marian Helper* magazine.

My stop in Rome that year was powerful. The Marians knew John Paul II well. Their priests and brothers regularly visited the pope, so when they found out I was going to be in Rome, they asked if I wanted to meet him. "Do you need to ask?" I replied. John Paul typically celebrated Mass in his private chapel at seven thirty in the morning. Bishops visiting Rome were welcome to join him. If any of the thirty-five seats in the tiny chapel were open and a layperson was "lucky" (blessed) enough to be on the list, they would call you the evening before. I prayed to Saint Thérèse of Lisieux for that blessing because she had met Pope Leo XIII when she visited Rome in 1887. My prayers were answered in spectacular fashion — my call came on the second-to-last day of my stay in Rome, on the centenary of Saint Thérèse's death, no less! And my first audience with John Paul II was on her feast day, October 1, 1997. After Mass, I presented him with recently published pages from the Marians' website, marian.org, of which I was the webmaster. The pages chronicled the pope's work advancing the cause of Sister Faustina Kowalska and the Divine Mercy message.

After that, I had nearly annual encounters with John Paul until 2002. During the pope's 1999 visit to the Basilica of Our Lady of Licheń in Poland, I stayed onsite with him and a sizable delegation of Marians from around the world. It was a rare treat to see the pope in his element — I was one of the few laypeople in the small group that greeted him upon his arrival. He bantered back and forth with the Marians in Polish, tossing out the occasional joke that had the men in stitches. It was two months after his birthday, but if memory serves me right, the men serenaded John Paul with the traditional Polish birthday song "Sto Lat," which roughly translates "One hundred years, one hundred years may you live!" With the centenary of the pope's birth approaching on May 18, 2020, that song takes on a whole new meaning.

The last time I saw him was eleven days after my wedding in 2002. I had seen him blessing the *sposi novelli* (newlyweds) during his weekly general audiences in Saint Peter's Square, and I had vowed that I would only marry a woman who desired such a blessing. A few months into our courtship, Michele raised the prospect of going to Rome for the blessing. That sealed the deal for me.

I was "lucky" (blessed) to have had five encounters with John Paul II, including three private audiences. It was life changing to have these brief moments with the perhaps most consequential pope of the past five hundred years — and the most visible human being who ever lived. I knew a great deal about John Paul before writing this book, but I discovered in my research that the breadth and depth of his influence was far more substantial than I had imagined. His work, his life, and his faith inspire me.

More than anything, John Paul lived for his relationship with Jesus Christ. His prayer life fueled everything he said and did. If there's one takeaway from this book, it's his call to prayer. Prayer is rocket fuel for sanctity, which he lived beautifully. As he told a gathering of young people in New Orleans in 1987, "If you really wish to follow Christ, if you want your love for him to grow and last, then you must be *faithful to prayer. It is the key to the vitality of your life in Christ.* Without prayer, your faith and love will die. If you are constant in daily prayer and in the Sunday celebration of Mass, your love for Jesus will increase. And your heart will know deep joy and peace, such as the world could never give."

This book looks at 100 ways Pope John Paul II influenced the world. The first ninety (#100 to #11) are grouped to best tell the story of how the Holy Father changed the world. The final ten (#10 to #1) are ranked according to importance based on conversations with scholars who knew and studied John Paul. Perhaps some will disagree with the rankings, but I expect that none will disagree that this extraordinary man left an indelible mark on the history of the Church — and the world!

100 **Religious Freedom.** From his youth, Karol Wojtyła understood that God created us for freedom. He also understood deeply the importance not only of freedom of worship but of freedom of religion. Modern secularists usually concede freedom of worship, confining faith to home and church buildings. Freedom of religion, however, brings faith into the public square. Wojtyła battled threats to freedom of religion from both the right and the left — first as a seminarian during the Nazi occupation of Poland and later as a priest, bishop, and pope facing the rise and spread of communism.

As a young bishop, he engaged in a public effort to defend religious liberty — freedom of religion — under communism, particularly in his work at Nowa Huta. He fought for twenty years to build a church in that Kraków suburb, which had been singled out by the communists to be a "workers' paradise." In 1977, his efforts prevailed when he consecrated the town's first church.

"When Nowa Huta was built with the intention that this would be a city without God, without a church, then Christ came here together with the people and through their lips spoke the fundamental truth about man," he said in his homily at the consecration Mass. "Man and his history cannot be reckoned by economic principles [alone], even according to the most exact rules of production and consumption. Man is greater than this. He is the image and likeness of God himself."

As pope, John Paul continued to battle for religious liberty. He addressed this theme in his 1988 World Day of Peace address, saying that "religious freedom, an essential requirement of the dignity of every person, is a cornerstone of the structure of human rights, and for this reason an irreplaceable factor in the good of individuals and of the whole of society, as well as of the personal fulfillment of each individual." He told the United Nations in 1995 that it must "safeguard *the fundamental right to freedom of religion and freedom of conscience*, as the cornerstones of the structure of human rights and the foundation of every truly free society. No one is permitted to suppress those rights by using coercive power to *impose an answer* to the mystery of man."

John Paul II was one of the twentieth century's foremost champions of religious freedom. Of his first meeting with Soviet leader Mikhail Gorbachev in 1989, political scientist Paul Kengor writes, the Holy Father "made many references to 'fundamental human rights,' including 'freedom of conscience, from which stems religious freedom.' He used the word *conscience* seven times in the dialogue. He also affirmed an individual's freedom of choice. 'A person becomes a believer through free choice; it is impossible to make someone believe.'"

99 **Dying with Dignity.** When this author met John Paul for the first time in 1997, the seventy-seven-year-old pope was healthy and walked to each person in the queue of about thirty people after his morning Mass in the papal apartments. At another meeting three years later, he sat in a chair as his guests approached him after Mass at Castel Gandolfo. The pope's physical health had begun to slip after a 1994 fall that fractured his femur; the decline happened slowly at first, but then more rapidly with each successive year.

John Paul showed the world how to die well. The news media captured his struggles to keep up with his duties as Supreme Pontiff while his health declined in the years leading up to his death in 2005. His lived witness was profound, lending poignancy to his teaching on the dignity of each human life, including the sick and dying. He railed against euthanasia and extolled the beauty of dying a natural death.

He wrote, "Even when not motivated by a selfish refusal to be burdened with the life of someone who is suffering, euthanasia must be called a false mercy, and indeed a disturbing 'perversion' of mercy. True 'compassion' leads to sharing another's pain; it does not kill the person whose suffering we cannot bear."

Human dignity, he taught, is an undeserved gift from God, not a status to be earned. Since the inherent dignity of each person flows from God, it is not ours to take away. John Paul gave his valuable time each Wednesday at the end of his general audience to bless those in wheelchairs, on crutches, and even on gurneys. That spoke volumes to the sick and dying — and to those of us who witnessed firsthand his love and compassion.

98 **The Shroud of Turin.** Just six weeks before his election to the Chair of Peter, Cardinal Wojtyła visited the Shroud of Turin during its five-week exhibition in Turin, in northern Italy. He visited for the first time as pope privately in 1980, returning in 1998 for a public visit during which he called the shroud a "mirror of the Gospel."

Some had expected him to pronounce the mysterious cloth that bears the image of a crucified man to be Jesus' authentic burial cloth. It had been the subject of an intense scientific study in 1978. While he acknowledged that the shroud had historically been an object of devotion, he noted that "since it is not a matter of faith, the Church has no specific competence to pronounce on these questions. She entrusts to scientists the task of continuing to investigate, so that satisfactory answers may be found to the questions connected with this Sheet."

He also noted that "the Shroud is a challenge to our intelligence. It first of all requires of every person, particularly the researcher, that he humbly grasp the profound message it sends to his reason and his life." He concluded by observing that the holy cloth "shows us Jesus at the moment of his greatest helplessness and reminds us that in the abasement of that death lies the salvation of the whole world. The Shroud thus becomes an invitation to face every experience … with the attitude of those who believe that God's merciful love overcomes every poverty, every limitation, every temptation to despair."

During a jubilee year address in 2000, he recalled his three visits to the shroud: "Each time was a profound experience of grace! For in the Man of the Shroud, God's infinite love *speaks to every human heart.*"

97 **Friendship with Padre Pio.** While here we have only one page dedicated to John Paul II and Saint Pio of Pietrelcina, certainly there is enough material to write many books. Padre Pio's fame had spread like wildfire after he received the stigmata — the wounds of Christ — in 1918, when he was thirty-one. In 1947, the newly ordained Father Wojtyła, who was studying in Rome, made a weeklong pilgrimage to visit the holy Franciscan priest in the small Italian town of San Giovanni Rotondo.

Rumors persisted for decades that Pio told Wojtyła that the Polish priest would become pope. After his election, however, according to the *Catholic Herald*, John Paul clarified that Pio had made no such prediction. But the holy Franciscan priest did tell him a secret: "When Fr. Wojtyla asked Padre Pio which one of his wounds (from the stigmata) caused him the most suffering, Padre Pio divulged, 'it is my shoulder wound, which no one knows about and has never been cured or treated.' ... Fr. Wojtyla was the only person that Padre Pio ever told about his most painful and bloody wound."

During a visit to Rome in 1962, Archbishop Wojtyła learned that one of his Polish friends was dying. He wrote to Pio, asking his intercession. The letter was hand-delivered to the friar, who reportedly replied: "I cannot say no to this request." Eleven days later, Wojtyła sent Pio a second letter thanking him for his intercession: "The lady who was ill with cancer was suddenly healed before entering the operating room."

John Paul canonized Pio in 2002, saying that the source of the holy friar's "spiritual fruitfulness can be found in that intimate and constant union with God, attested to by his long hours spent in prayer and in the confessional. He loved to repeat, 'I am a poor Franciscan who prays,' convinced that 'prayer is the best weapon we have, a key that opens the heart of God.'"

96 **Visits to the United States.** John Paul II had a special affinity for the United States of America. This affinity is evident not only in his speeches and writings on the national values of freedom and justice contained in the nation's founding documents but in his love for Americans themselves. Prior to his election as pope in 1978, he visited the United States twice — in 1969 and again in 1976 — as archbishop of Kraków.

As pope, he visited the United States seven times, including two brief stopovers in Alaska. His five significant visits were packed with joy, drama, and record-setting crowds. John Paul extolled the Founders' vision of freedom and self-rule, but he reminded Americans of the responsibility that comes with liberty. "Every generation of Americans needs to know that freedom consists not in doing what we like, but in having the right to do what we ought," he said on a 1995 visit.

Poignantly, it was during his six-city 1979 visit that he best expressed his love and challenge for the United States. When he departed New York, he said, "My final prayer is this: that God will bless America so that she may increasingly become, and truly be and long remain, 'one nation, under God, indivisible, with liberty and justice for all.'" Similarly, he told Bostonians, "America has opened her heart to me. And on my part, I come to you — America — with sentiments of friendship, reverence and esteem. I come as one who already knows you and loves you, as one who wishes you to fulfill completely your noble destiny of service to the world. Once again I can now admire firsthand the beauty of this vast land stretching between two oceans; once again I am experiencing the warm hospitality of the American people."

95 **End Times.** There's no way to talk about John Paul II and the end times without mentioning Fátima (#85), Divine Mercy (#2), and Saint Faustina (#28), to whom Jesus appeared, asking her to prepare the world for his final coming. In his second encyclical, *Dives in Misericordia* ("Rich in Mercy"), John Paul urges us "to implore God's mercy for humanity in this hour of history, ... to beg for it at this difficult, critical phase of the history of the Church."

As Vicar of Christ, he knew it was his job to read the signs of the times and to interpret what the Holy Spirit was saying to the Church. But even before taking his seat on the throne of Peter, he was a prophetic voice. As a delegate to Philadelphia's Eucharistic Congress in 1976, Cardinal Wojtyła said, "We are now standing in the face of the greatest historical confrontation humanity has gone through. I do not think that wide circles of the American society or wide circles of the Christian community realize this fully. We are now facing the final confrontation between the Church and the anti-Church, of the Gospel versus the anti-Gospel, between Christ and the antichrist."

There isn't room here to unpack this powerful statement, but it is consistent with John Paul's statements on Fátima and with his remarks to a small group of German bishops in 1980: "We must prepare ourselves to suffer great trials before long. ... With your and my prayer, it is possible to mitigate this tribulation, but it is no longer possible to avert it, because only thus can the Church be effectively renewed. ... We must be strong and prepared, and trust in Christ and His Mother, and be very, very assiduous in praying the Rosary."

94 **Admiration for Archbishop Fulton Sheen.** Everyone who grew up in the United States during the 1940s, '50s, and '60s knew who Fulton Sheen was. He was among the world's first media evangelists — first on radio, then on television, where he became one of the most watched people in America. He had such broad appeal — including winning an Emmy Award for Most Outstanding Personality in 1953 — that a young actor named Martin Estevez changed his name to Martin Sheen. According to one scholar, "There was no more effective Catholic apologist in the United States, teaching and preaching on every aspect of the faith, but he was especially effective in dissecting atheistic communism."

What does this have to do with John Paul II? Cardinal Wojtyła, too, was taken with Sheen, so much so that he studied the American bishop's cadence and speaking style, incorporating it into his approach to speaking in English. The two men met but once, just two months before Sheen's death. John Paul was in New York for a morning Mass on October 2, 1979. "As Sheen's biographer Thomas Reeves described it, the 'feeble' Sheen made his way to the Holy Father in the sanctuary and fell to his knees before him. John Paul II humbly lifted him up, hugged him and thanked him for having 'written and spoken well of the Lord Jesus.' He told his grateful servant that he had been a 'loyal son of the Church.'"

Later that month, John Paul wrote Sheen a formal letter. Sheen, in return, wrote the Holy Father an extremely moving missive, essentially predicting greatness for this new pope. It's certainly within the realm of possibility that Sheen, one of the world's foremost critics of socialism and communism, knew that John Paul would help bring down the Soviet empire.

93 **Relations with Islam.** Many John Paul II admirers are disturbed to learn that he kissed the Quran in 1999. There's no official explanation for why he did so. Some saw it as a betrayal, while others interpreted it as a gesture of peace toward the guests who presented it to him.

The important thing to bear in mind is that the pope made a great effort to improve the Church's relations with Islam. In early 2001, during a visit to Syria, he became the first pope to enter and pray in a mosque, where he said, "For all the times that Muslims and Christians have offended one another, we need to seek forgiveness from the Almighty and to offer each other forgiveness."

However, John Paul was a forceful voice condemning the 9/11 terror attacks. He understood Islam well: "Islam is not a religion of redemption. There is no room for the Cross and the Resurrection. … For this reason, not only the theology but also the anthropology of Islam is very distant from Christianity." He was also firm with the United States and its allies in the wake of 9/11 about the need to refrain from war. During a visit to Kazakhstan less than two weeks after 9/11, John Paul called for peace: "I invite both Christians and Muslims to raise an intense prayer to the One, Almighty God whose children we all are, that the supreme good of peace may reign in the world. May people everywhere, strengthened by divine wisdom, work for a civilization of love, in which there is no room for hatred, discrimination or violence."

Three years later, he hosted the Papal Concert of Reconciliation, broadcast worldwide from the Vatican. And the new *Catechism* (#5) he published notes that "together with us they [Muslims] adore the one, merciful God, mankind's judge on the last day" (CCC 841).

92 **World Peace.** Pope Saint Paul VI established January 1 as the World Day of Peace in 1967, and John Paul ensured that the day became known worldwide as an opportunity to draw mankind together. One scholar observes that although John Paul "did not leave a peace encyclical, he did leave a comprehensive peace agenda that he developed over the course of his more than twenty-six-year pontificate." He preached peace in his writings, World Day of Peace messages, addresses to diplomatic corps and heads of state, three addresses to the United Nations, and more.

At the heart of the Holy Father's peace initiatives is the core Christian teaching on the inherent dignity of the human person. During his 1979 visit to Ireland, he urged an end to Catholic-Protestant violence, which was rampant at the time: "To all who bear political responsibility for the affairs of Ireland … you must show that there is a peaceful, political way to justice. You must show that peace achieves the works of justice, and violence does not."

He spoke out often against conflict, including the First Gulf War, the conflict in Bosnia, and the violence sparked by apartheid in South Africa. A vocal opponent of the 2003 United States–led Iraq War, John Paul challenged leaders to seek a peaceful solution: "'*NO TO WAR!*' War is not always inevitable. It is always a defeat for humanity." He sent an envoy to meet with President George W. Bush, and he called on the United Nations to mediate the conflict. His efforts led to speculation that he would receive the 2003 Nobel Peace Prize, which was ultimately awarded to Shirin Ebadi, an Iranian attorney/judge and noted human rights advocate.

"Do not be afraid to take a chance on peace, to teach peace," John Paul wrote. "Peace will be the last word of history."

91 **Impact on Poland.** Entire books have been written on John Paul II's passion for his homeland. He certainly left a deep and lasting impact on Poland. Before he became pope — as a priest, bishop, and cardinal — Wojtyła was already a national hero. Poles loved him for his solid teaching, his passion for young people, and his resistance to the communist government's efforts to minimize the Church in Poland. As pope, he led the charge for religious freedom and made the first crack in the Iron Curtain (#4).

Today, visitors to Poland find devotion to John Paul everywhere. One American visitor observed, "In the main square of his hometown of Wadowice, there's a larger than life statue of the pope with holy water springing from the ground beneath his feet. In Wroclaw, the Pope is immortalized in stained glass in a church where he once gave a speech. Every church in Poland has at least one portrait of the Virgin Mary, but every important church has a portrait of the Virgin Mary wearing a golden crown placed on her head by John Paul II."

As pope, he made nine apostolic journeys — pilgrimages — to Poland. The first and most impactful was his 1979 visit (#30). Fittingly, his final visit to Poland, in 2002, was for the consecration of the new Shrine of The Divine Mercy in Kraków. And more than two million Poles flocked to Rome in 2005 to honor their hero by attending his funeral.

The Holy Father awoke in the Polish people a sense of solidarity and a desire for freedom. According to Mateusz Morawiecki, who was elected Poland's prime minister in 2017, "He brought to Poland something exceptional at a time of huge and deep divisions."

90 **Letter to Artists.** One of John Paul's most read, quoted, and studied documents is his 1999 Letter to Artists. As a poet, a playwright, and an actor himself, he understood well the artist's heart. In 1939, Germany invaded Poland. It was a bleak time in Poland's history. A nineteen-year-old Karol Wojtyła and some friends founded a clandestine group to pray, read, write, and act. Decades later, the pope would write to artists, "In so far as it seeks the beautiful, fruit of an imagination which rises above the everyday, art is by its nature a kind of appeal to the mystery. Even when they explore the darkest depths of the soul or the most unsettling aspects of evil, artists give voice in a way to the universal desire for redemption."

His letter invites those with creative talent to use their gifts to serve both the Church and the world: "Those who perceive in themselves this kind of divine spark which is the artistic vocation — as poet, writer, sculptor, architect, musician, actor and so on — feel at the same time the obligation not to waste this talent but to develop it, in order to put it at the service of their neighbour and of humanity as a whole." John Paul wanted artists to know that they are to reflect God in their creative endeavors.

Even nonartists, he wrote, are called to make something beautiful for the Lord. His challenge extends to everyone to offer their lives to the Lord. "All men and women are entrusted with the task of crafting their own life: in a certain sense, they are to make of it a work of art, a masterpiece."

For John Paul, art and beauty are inseparable. "The artist has a special relationship to beauty. In a very true sense it can be said that beauty is the vocation bestowed on him by the Creator in the gift of 'artistic talent.' And, certainly, this too is a talent which ought to be made to bear fruit, in keeping with the sense of the Gospel parable of the talents."

His Letter to Artists outlines the relationship between art and faith — and the relationship of beauty, goodness, and truth — as well as our responsibility to an "artistic vocation in the service of beauty." Beauty is necessary for evangelization. Because beauty lifts the soul to God, he warns, artists have a unique responsibility: "The particular vocation of individual artists decides the arena in which they serve and points as well to the tasks they must assume, the hard work they must endure and the responsibility they must accept. Artists who are conscious of all this know too that they must labour without allowing themselves to be driven by the search for empty glory or the craving for cheap popularity, and still less by the calculation of some possible profit for themselves."

89 **Theater.** John Paul II had a flair for the dramatic. Naturally charismatic, he drew people in with the way he carried himself, the way he stood and moved. He honed these gifts as a young man on the stage in Poland and used them throughout his life to communicate the Gospel on the world stage. His early ambition was to be an actor. In the fall of 1939, he entered Kraków's Jagiellonian University, where he joined an avant-garde student theater troupe. Then came the German invasion, which pushed his theatrical pursuits underground. He later described himself as "completely absorbed by a passion for literature, especially dramatic literature, and for the theater."

He wrote five plays — most notably *The Jeweler's Shop* in 1960 while he was auxiliary bishop of Kraków; it was subtitled *A Meditation on the Sacrament of Matrimony, Passing on Occasion into a Drama*. Biographer George Weigel writes that "theater, for Wojtyła, was also an experience of community, the self-disciplined action of a group of individuals who, by blending their individual talents with the talents of others, become something more than the sum of their parts. ... If drama could unveil the deeper dimensions of the truth of things, might there be a dramatic structure to every human life? To the whole of reality?"

John Paul believed deeply that "mine is an invitation to rediscover the depth of the spiritual and religious dimension which has been typical of art in its noblest forms in every age. ... [Christian artists] are invited to use your creative intuition to enter into the heart of the mystery of the Incarnate God and at the same time into the mystery of man."

88 **Poetry.** Among this author's most treasured possessions is a copy of *The Place Within: The Poetry of Pope John Paul II*, signed by John Paul on July 31, 1998. I used to own a signed deluxe edition with a slipcover, a gift from a friend with connections to the papal household. But then came a call from the Vatican in 1999: the pope did not have a deluxe version in his private library and was requesting *my* copy. I couldn't say no. In return, they sent me a "lowly" hardcover version — along with the knowledge that my deluxe edition made it into John Paul's personal library.

Wojtyła began writing poetry as a university student in 1939, often using pseudonyms. He continued writing poems well into his papacy, but they weren't widely published until after he became pope. Among his topics were nature, faith, love, war, and death. His poems paid homage to his mother, who died when he was nine, but they always returned to the Eucharist as the source and summit of the Catholic faith.

According to biographer George Weigel, "Like his plays, Wojtyła's poetry is a way of 'being present' to others in a conversation about the truth of things. It is not easy poetry, in the original or in translation. Yet his poems display the 'voice' of Karol Wojtyła in a privileged way, particularly his insight into human relationships, the struggles of the individual conscience, and the mystical experience."

The arts were central to John Paul's pontificate, but he had a special place in his heart for poetry. In his 1979 address to the United Nations, he underscored the value of poetry: "This truth [of the value of sharing spiritual goods] is confirmed, for example, by the works of creativity — I mean by the works of thought, poetry, music, and the figurative arts, fruits of man's spirit."

87 Friendship with Cardinal Stefan Wyszyński. Cardinal Stefan Wyszyński was one of John Paul II's greatest heroes and mentors, perhaps second only to his own father. Wyszyński served as bishop of Lublin from 1946 to 1948 (while the future pope studied at the Catholic University of Lublin) and as archbishop of Warsaw from 1948 to 1981. As the top leader (primate) of the Church in Poland, Wyszyński stood firm against the communist government, earning credit for preserving the Faith in the face of repression and persecution. He was imprisoned for three years and is considered a national hero.

Wyszyński and Wojtyła met in 1958 when Wyszyński summoned the young priest to inform him that he was the new auxiliary bishop of Kraków. Six years later, Wojtyła became Kraków's new archbishop with Wyszyński's blessing, despite his not having been one of Wyszyński's top picks. Wyszyński served as Wojtyła's mentor and spiritual father through the 1960s and '70s, and he reportedly championed Wojtyła's candidacy in both 1978 papal conclaves.

The first time the two met after John Paul's election became one of the most touching moments of his pontificate. The Polish cardinal approached the new pope to kiss his ring in Saint Peter's Square on the day of his inauguration, but John Paul quickly rose, embraced his mentor, and kissed his cheek. Hundreds of statues across Poland commemorate the moment.

During a 1999 trip to Poland where he faced a grueling itinerary of twenty-one cities in thirteen days, John Paul revealed a prophecy given him by Wyszyński. Shortly after his election to the papacy in 1978, Wyszyński told him, "If God has chosen you, he has chosen you to lead the Church into the next millennium."

86 Solidarity (*Solidarność*) **Trade Union.** The Holy Father's first visit to Poland in 1979 was the first crack in the Iron Curtain (#4), and it sent shock waves through the entire Soviet Union. Perhaps the visit's most visible impact was the formation of the first independent labor union in the Soviet bloc: *Solidarność* (Solidarity), founded in 1980 at the Lenin Shipyard in Gdańsk. According to one Polish historian, "Solidarity became a nation-wide movement that clearly identified itself with John Paul II. It was no coincidence that the Gdańsk Shipyard's entrance gate, with its John Paul II's [*sic*] portrait, became the movement's symbol. In this sense, the Pope took part in the overthrow of communism, though not as a political actor but rather as an initiator of an ethical movement."

In the union's clandestine years, the pope and the United States provided roughly $50 million to Solidarity's efforts. John Paul also championed its work via his writing and public speaking. Kenneth Zagacki writes that "the Pope was motivated by a belief that Catholicism and the individual conscience stood diametrically opposed to Communism's suppression of religious, economic and political freedoms, which established the state as an alternative to a higher being." In *Sollicitudo Rei Socialis*, his 1987 encyclical on labor, John Paul further develops Church teaching on the concept of solidarity with the poor and marginalized as a constitutive element of the Gospel. The document, which insists that development must contribute to the fullness of being human, bolstered Solidarity's efforts.

Most historians and scholars agree that John Paul played an essential role in the creation of the Solidarity labor movement, "which … led to the collapse of communism in Poland, and that, in turn, initiated the sequential collapses of the communist governments of Eastern Europe from East Germany to Bulgaria."

85 **Our Lady of Fátima.** John Paul II had a tremendous devotion to the Blessed Mother (#10). For numerous reasons, her apparitions at Fátima had special meaning to him. First, one of the Fátima visionaries, Sister Lucia, was still alive during his pontificate, and they met during each of the pope's three visits to Fátima. Second, the attempt on his life (#84) occurred on the feast of Our Lady of Fátima. Finally, the "third secret of Fátima" related directly to that event.

On May 13, 1917, Our Lady appeared to three shepherd children near the town of Fátima, Portugal. Exactly sixty-four years later, a gunman opened fire on John Paul in Saint Peter's Square. Two bullets lodged in his abdomen, another struck his finger, and a fourth hit his right arm. Commenting on his miraculous survival, the Holy Father gave credit to Our Lady of Fátima, famously stating that "one hand pulled the trigger, and another guided the bullet." The bullet that lodged closest to his heart was removed and welded into the crown of Mary's statue in Fátima.

John Paul made three visits to Fátima: on the first anniversary of the assassination attempt, on the tenth anniversary, and in 2000 when he beatified the child visionaries Jacinta and Francisco. This final visit, which emphasized the significance of Our Lady's message for our day, was significant, as he made few foreign trips that year because of all the jubilee year events in Rome. After the beatification Mass for Francisco and Jacinta, it was announced that the third secret of Fátima spoke of a "bishop in white" being killed upon a great mountain of martyrs. John Paul and Sister Lucia interpreted the secret as referring to the 1981 attempt on his life.

84 **Surviving Assassination.** Dozens of popes — including the first, Saint Peter — have been martyred. Nearly a dozen others were murdered, but it's been more than seven hundred years since a pope died a violent death. That nearly changed on May 13, 1981, when Turkish assassin Mehmet Ali Ağca opened fire on John Paul II in Saint Peter's Square.

Ağca had arrived in Rome three days before the shooting. He later told investigators that he met with three accomplices in Rome, with instructions from Zilo Vassilev, a Bulgarian military attaché in Italy. Ağca and backup gunman Oral Çelik were to shoot the pope and escape to the Bulgarian embassy under the cover of the panic generated by a small explosion. After Ağca fired at the pope, a nun, bystanders, and Vatican security chief Camillo Cibin grabbed him. Çelik fled without setting off his bomb.

John Paul, who was nearly sixty-one at the time, required emergency surgery when he arrived at the Agostino Gemelli University Polyclinic. He had lost a great deal of blood and was in cardiac arrest, which was successfully defibrillated. One bullet had passed through his body, puncturing the intestines, necessitating nearly six hours of surgery and a colostomy.

According to a news report, "He was released from the hospital three weeks [after the shooting] but went back on June 20 after suffering a debilitating virus infection. On August 5, he underwent a second operation to reverse the colostomy." He walked out of the hospital on August 15. His complete recovery necessitated two operations and nearly five months of convalescence. John Paul attributed his survival to Our Lady of Fátima. He forgave his assailant and visited him in prison.

83   **Forgiving Mehmet Ali Ağca.** A great deal of mystery and intrigue still surround Mehmet Ali Ağca, the man who attempted to kill John Paul II in 1981. During interrogation, he suggested that the KGB ordered the hit, but he later recanted. He had killed a Turkish journalist and was imprisoned for that crime less than three months before he shot the pope. He escaped from prison and headed to Rome in May 1981. The Holy Father asked the world from his hospital bed to "pray for my brother … whom I have sincerely forgiven." He then lobbied the Italian president to pardon him. The pardon came in June 2000. But what most intrigued the world was John Paul's visit with Ağca in prison in 1983.

The two met in Ağca's cell in Rome's Rebibbia Prison. They spoke privately, seated close together in a corner of the cell. Ağca kissed John Paul's hand, and they talked for twenty-one minutes. As John Paul rose to leave, he gave Ağca a rosary in silver and mother-of-pearl. After the event, many were astounded to learn that Ağca had not been handcuffed and that his cell door had been left ajar. A Vatican photographer captured the event at the pope's request to show the world that forgiveness and mercy are possible in a fallen world.

"The Lord has given me the grace to let us meet as men, as brothers, because all the events of our lives must confirm that God is our father, and we are all his children in Jesus Christ," John Paul said. Ağca served nineteen years in an Italian prison before the pardon. Italy then deported him to Turkey, where he served a ten-year sentence. In 2007, he converted to Roman Catholicism. He was released from jail in 2010.

82 **Friendship with Ronald Reagan.** Of all the world leaders John Paul II interacted with during his twenty-six-year papacy, he had a special kinship with President Ronald Reagan. Both men sought to end the Cold War, both survived assassination attempts in 1981, and both had fathers who died in 1941. As young men, both had suffered serious illnesses or injuries, and both were athletes and talented actors.

More than that, Reagan and John Paul genuinely liked one another. They met for the first time at the Vatican in 1982. During that first meeting, they confided in each other their conviction that God had spared their lives for the purpose of defeating communism (#4). Two years later, "the Holy See and the United States announced the establishment of full diplomatic relations, repealing the 1867 congressional legislation which had cut off all funding for an American representative to the Vatican."

They saw each other again in 1984 in Alaska, then twice in 1987 — once at the Vatican and once in Miami, where Reagan welcomed the pope back to America. Beyond the meetings, there was a tremendous amount of intelligence sharing, with envoys flying back and forth between Rome and Washington for secret meetings. Many of the related documents remain classified to this day.

The two men's camaraderie was obvious to the cameras. Then in 1989, two Solidarity members and two Polish Americans visited ex-President Reagan. They asked Reagan for words of political wisdom for the Solidarity members. "Listen to your conscience," he said, "because that is where the Holy Spirit speaks to you." Reagan then pointed to a picture of John Paul: "He is my best friend. Yes, you know I'm Protestant, but he's still my best friend."

81 **Friendship with Mother Teresa.** It's not often that a pope has the opportunity to beatify his friend. But shortly after Mother Teresa's death in 1997, John Paul waived the five-year waiting period to begin her canonization process.

The pair shared a remarkable history, meeting for the first time in 1973 at the Fortieth World Eucharistic Congress in Australia; Cardinal Wojtyła mentioned the meeting in his personal diary. The future saints intersected again in 1976 at another Eucharistic congress, this time in Philadelphia. Wrote one historian, "As odd as it may seem, neither was much known yet in the Catholic world. But their speeches resonated. Mother Teresa addressed physical hunger and love of small things, Cardinal Wojtyla focused on a different form of hunger — the hunger for freedom."

Mother Teresa had a profound impact on the pope. During his ten-day visit to India in 1986, she famously climbed uninvited into the popemobile and kissed his ring. John Paul, in return, kissed the top of the nun's head. He then visited Nirmal Hriday, the home for the poor she founded in 1952. The pair "stopped at each of the eighty-six patients, spoon-feeding the sick and the dying. At the end of his visit, he said: 'Nirmal Hriday is a place of hope, a house built on courage and faith.'" Mother called it the best day of her life.

The pair remained fast friends throughout the years, and when he beatified the Albanian-born nun in 2003, he extolled her tenacity: "Let us praise the Lord for this *diminutive woman in love with God*, a humble Gospel messenger and a tireless benefactor of humanity. In her we honour one of the most important figures of our time. Let us welcome her message and follow her example."

80 **Visits to Mexico.** As pope, John Paul II made 104 foreign trips, visiting Mexico five times — more than any other country except France, Poland, and the United States. The first foreign visit of his pontificate, in January 1979, began with a six-day tour of Mexico, where more than ten million people came out to see him. He forever captured the hearts of the Mexican people by donning a sombrero, stooping to kiss the tarmac on his arrival, and becoming the first pontiff to visit Mexico and its most famous shrine, the Basilica of Our Lady of Guadalupe.

At the time, Mexico was officially an anticlerical country. Masons were in control of the government and operated at the highest levels in the business community. The people, however, yearned for freedom and embraced the Polish pope. According to Cardinal Stanisław Dziwisz, "Huge crowds poured into the streets. The chant that later became famous throughout the world also made its debut: *'Juan Pablo Segundo, te quiere todo el mundo'* (John Paul II, the whole world loves you). Happily surprised, Karol Wojtyła abandoned himself to what was an almost-smothering embrace."

Officially, the 1979 visit centered on the Third General Conference of Latin American and Caribbean Bishops. The conference emphasized the Church's preferential option for the poor. "When injustices grow worse and the distance between rich and poor increases distressingly, the social doctrine, in a form which is creative and open to the broad fields of the Church's presence, must be a valuable instrument for formation and action," John Paul told the bishops.

The trip also had its share of politics. The pope drew the ire of the KGB by pushing back against "liberation theology" and pointing out in his address the "anthropological error" of Marxism. In addition, "at the time, the Vatican and Mexico had no diplomatic relations, so the pope hadn't been formally 'invited' by the government. Throughout the trip, John Paul II broke the law by wearing a cassock in public (the bishops who greeted him at the airport were in coats and ties)." The Holy Father's visits and subsequent diplomacy resulted in a thaw between the Holy See and Mexico. In 1992, Mexico reestablished formal diplomatic relations with the Vatican after more than 130 years.

The "pilgrim pope" returned to Mexico in 1990, 1993, 1999, and 2002. On his final visit, he canonized Juan Diego Cuauhtlatoatzin, the native peasant to whom Our Lady appeared four times in 1531. His canonization made Juan Diego the first native of the Americas to be declared a saint. During his own 2012 visit to Mexico, Pope Benedict XVI remarked, "Now I can understand why Pope John Paul II said: 'I feel I am a Mexican Pope.'"

79 **Our Lady of Guadalupe.** The Holy Father had a great devotion to the Virgin of Guadalupe, who is credited with the conversion of Mexico in the sixteenth century. "You, Mother of Guadalupe, have entered decisively into the Christian life of the people of Mexico," he said during his 1979 visit to the Mexican basilica. "No less has been your presence in other places, where your children invoke you with tender names ... names by which in each nation and even in each region the peoples of Latin America express their most profound devotion to you."

So great was his devotion to Our Lady of Guadalupe that he transformed a grotto under Saint Peter's Basilica to honor her. The chapel includes a mosaic depicting her image on Juan Diego's tilma. "Mexico, which stands out for its fidelity to the Pope, wanted to bear witness, with this beautiful chapel of Our Lady of Guadalupe in the center of Christianity, not only to its Marian vocation, but also to its historical roots and the unifying force of its culture, which enriches the whole Church," he said at the chapel's 1992 dedication.

During his 1999 visit to Mexico, he declared that the Feast of Our Lady of Guadalupe would be celebrated in every church in the Americas. He entrusted "the future of the continent to ... [the] Holy Virgin of Guadalupe" and asked her to "teach everyone, political leaders and citizens, to live in true freedom and to act according to the requirements of justice and respect for human rights, so that peace may thus be established once and for all. To you, O Lady of Guadalupe, Mother of Jesus and our Mother, belong all the love, honour, glory and endless praise of your American sons and daughters!"

78 **Social Justice.** In a 1993 audience, John Paul II said that "Jesus formulated the precept of mutual love, which implies respect for every person and his rights. It implies rules of social justice aimed at recognizing what is each person's due and at harmoniously sharing earthly goods among individuals, families and groups."

For John Paul, social justice and peace went hand in hand. The *Catechism of the Catholic Church* (#5), which he promulgated in 1992, says, "Society ensures social justice when it provides the conditions that allow associations or individuals to obtain what is their due, according to their nature and their vocation. … Social justice can be obtained only in respecting the transcendent dignity of man" (CCC 1928–29).

However, like many phrases in Church parlance, "social justice" has gotten a bad rap. For many, it has come to be associated with felt banners, guitar Masses, and liberation theology. And some social justice leaders in Catholic circles have put their energies behind labor unions, just wages, and women's rights while neglecting the unfettered slaughter of millions of unborn children — certainly the greatest social justice crisis in human history.

John Paul placed the plight of the unborn front and center in his teaching on social justice. "Today there exists a great multitude of weak and defenceless human beings, unborn children in particular, whose fundamental right to life is being trampled upon," he taught in 1995. "If, at the end of the last century, the Church could not be silent about the injustices of those times, still less can she be silent today, when the social injustices of the past, unfortunately not yet overcome, are being compounded in many regions of the world by still more grievous forms of injustice and oppression, even if these are being presented as elements of progress in view of a new world order."

77 Denunciation of Liberation Theology.

From the beginning of his pontificate, the Holy Father built a case against liberation theology, which emphasizes liberation from social, political, and economic oppression as an anticipation of ultimate salvation. Most strains of liberation theology apply Marxist economic theory to the Gospel. John Paul believed "that religion must transcend politics, and that the primacy of the spiritual can be surrendered by no Christianity worthy of the name."

John Paul pushed back hard against liberation theology when he spoke to Mexico's bishops in 1979. "This idea of Christ as a political figure, a revolutionary, as the subversive man from Nazareth, does not tally with the Church's catechesis," he said. Rather than subscribe to the liberation of man via political means, John Paul taught that man's greatest struggle should be the liberation from sin. Quoting Pope Saint Paul VI to Mexico's bishops, he said that Christ's salvation is "liberation from everything that oppresses man, but which is, above all, liberation from sin and the Evil One." With John Paul's approval, the Congregation for the Doctrine of the Faith went further in 1984, stating, "To put one's trust in violent means in the hope of restoring more justice is to become the victim of a fatal illusion: violence begets violence and degrades man."

During his 1983 visit to Nicaragua, John Paul II famously chastised Father Ernesto Cardenal Martínez publicly because of the priest's adherence to liberation theology and his involvement in the leftist revolutionary Sandinista government of Nicaragua, which was restricting the Church.

The pope's efforts slowed the movement's progress in Latin America and beyond. Liberation theology has waned, but it continues to influence Catholics. It has, unfortunately, driven many from the Faith. It preaches political — and even armed — solutions to help the poor break free from the bonds of oppression, particularly in nations governed by dictators.

76 **Stand against Socialism.** John Paul II was a critic of "unbridled capitalism." Economic systems, he taught in his 1991 encyclical *Centesimus Annus*, must "provide all individuals and nations with the basic conditions which will enable them to share in development." However, he railed against socialism as an errant philosophy:

> The fundamental error of socialism is anthropological in nature. Socialism considers the individual person simply as an element, a molecule within the social organism, so that the good of the individual is completely subordinated to the functioning of the socio-economic mechanism. Socialism likewise maintains that the good of the individual can be realized without reference to his free choice, to the unique and exclusive responsibility which he exercises in the face of good or evil. Man is thus reduced to a series of social relationships, and the concept of the person as the autonomous subject of moral decisions disappears, the very subject whose decisions build the social order.

John Paul II had lived under socialism and understood how it corrupted the working class. He saw Pope Leo XIII as a prophetic voice in the late 1800s. On the one hundredth anniversary of Leo XIII's *Rerum Novarum* (1891), John Paul reiterated the Catholic condemnation of socialism: "It may seem surprising that 'socialism' appeared at the beginning of [Pope Leo's] critique of solutions to the 'question of the working class' at a time when 'socialism' was not yet in the form of a strong and powerful State, with all the resources which that implies, as was later to happen. However, he correctly judged the danger posed to the masses by the attractive presentation of this simple and radical solution to the 'question of the working class.'"

75 **Meeting with Dictators.** Much to the chagrin of his critics, John Paul met with several dictators during his pontificate. He was the first pope to set foot in Cuba (#51), meeting with Fidel Castro in 1998. Doubtless, the Holy Father was hoping for the same Holy Spirit moment that happened during his first visit to Poland in 1979 (#30).

"May Cuba, with all its magnificent possibilities, open itself to the world," he said at the welcome ceremony in Havana in January 1998, *"and may the world open itself up to Cuba."* The pope's presence electrified the island nation, held captive by Castro's ruthless dictatorship since the 1950s, but it inspired only small changes. According to a news report, by 2015 "Christmas [was] recognized as a religious holiday in Cuba. … But some of the goals the pope set for the church during that visit — like the right to religious education or obtaining access to radio or television airtime — [had] not been fulfilled."

John Paul also hoped for the spark of freedom during his 1987 visit to Chile, then under the dictatorship of General Augusto Pinochet. The pilgrimage carried the slogan *El amor es más fuerte* ("Love Is Stronger"). The pope made it clear from the outset that his trip was designed to restore democracy to Chile. One historian writes that when John Paul met with the dictator, Pinochet asked him: "Why is the Church always talking about democracy? One method of government is as good as another." The pope shot back, "No. The people have a right to their liberties, even if they make mistakes in exercising them." Pinochet, a Catholic, took John Paul's counsel to heart: "By October of the following year, Pinochet organized a plebiscite asking the Chilean people if they wanted Pinochet to extend his rule by another eight years or if they wanted a return to civilian rule. They chose the latter option."

74 **The Popemobile.** While John Paul didn't own the first popemobile, he certainly made it famous. In fact, the term didn't come into common parlance until his 1979 visit to Ireland. Prior to John Paul II's papacy, the Holy Father was generally carried aloft by twelve footmen (*palafrenieri*) on a ceremonial throne, or *sedia gestatoria*. Such thrones were mainly used to carry popes to and from papal ceremonies in the Basilica of Saint John Lateran and Saint Peter's Basilica.

The first car designed exclusively for a pope was a Mercedes-Benz Nürburg 460 Pullman given to Pope Pius XI by the German car manufacturer in 1930. When Paul VI visited New York in 1965, he used a custom-built 1964 Lehmann-Peterson Lincoln Continental. Later, he used a Mercedes-Benz 600 Pullman-Landaulet. John Paul I, during his thirty-three-day pontificate, rode in a black limousine.

John Paul II used a variety of automobiles during his twenty-six-year papacy; the vehicles varied from country to country. During his famous 1979 visit to Poland (#30), his ride was an FSC Star 660. The massive six-wheeler was essentially a converted firetruck. He toured Ireland in a highly modified 1979 Ford Transit — painted bright yellow no less!

Popemobiles became more secure after John Paul was shot in 1981 while riding in the back of an open Fiat Campagnola. On his tour of the United Kingdom in 1982, he used a bombproof, four-wheel-drive Land Rover and a massive Leyland Constructor 6540cc. By 2002, he was riding in a customized Mercedes-Benz G-Wagen with nearly 360-degree views and extra lighting so the pope could be seen at night. Despite the popularity of the term, John Paul in 2002 asked journalists to stop calling his vehicle the popemobile because he thought it sounded "undignified." He lost that battle.

73 **Visits to Canada.** John Paul II played a huge role in this author's faith journey, particularly because of his historic 1984 visit to my native land, Canada. Few Canadians are aware that Wojtyła also toured Canada in 1969 when he was cardinal archbishop of Kraków, stopping to preach in Québec City, Ottawa, Calgary, Edmonton, Winnipeg, Toronto, Hamilton, London, Yellowknife, and Saint Catharines.

During his 1984 visit, John Paul preached to nearly a million people, delivered thirty-four major addresses, and covered more than nine thousand miles. "Your fervour is the sign that the message of the Successor of Peter, who has come to bear witness to Jesus Christ, has found men and women ready to work for a new world," he said in his farewell address.

He had planned a stop in Fort Simpson, Northwest Territories, but heavy fog prevented his plane from landing. In 1987, however, breaking from an existing US visit, he made good on his promise to visit the village. He told those gathered to hear him, "The soul of the native peoples of Canada is hungry for the Spirit of God, because it is hungry for justice, peace, love, goodness, fortitude, responsibility and human dignity. ... Be assured that the Church will walk that path with you."

He returned to Canada in 2002 for World Youth Day in Toronto. Sadly, it was his final appearance at the jubilant youth gathering he had founded. At the July 27 vigil, after pilgrims had prayed the Liturgy of the Hours, thousands of young people waited silently. John Paul II asked them: "On what foundations, on what certainties should we build our lives and the life of the community to which we belong?" And then he answered: "*Christ alone is the cornerstone* on which it is possible solidly to build one's existence. Only Christ — known, contemplated and loved — is the faithful friend who never lets us down, who becomes our travelling companion, and whose words warm our hearts."

72 **His Longevity.** Saint Peter's Basilica is the world's largest Catholic church building, and it is likely that the basilica's namesake will always be the longest-serving pontiff. Saint Peter is thought to have served thirty-seven years, from approximately A.D. 30 to 67. Second comes Pius IX (1846–1878), whose reign lasted thirty-one years, seven months, and twenty-three days. John Paul II is third at twenty-six years, five months, and eighteen days (9,665 days). Interestingly, his pontificate immediately followed one of the shortest reigns in history — John Paul I's thirty-three-day stint as pope.

Why is his longevity important? For the simple reason that his years of service allowed him a profound influence in terms of the breadth of his teaching, his world travel (#12), the number of bishops he appointed (#22), the number of saints he canonized (#15), and the number of souls he touched.

In fact, the Holy Father broached the subject of longevity several times — memorably in his 2005 message for Lent, mere months before his death at nearly eighty-five years of age. Quoting from Deuteronomy, he said, "'*Loving the Lord ... means life to you, and length of days.*' ... According to the Biblical understanding, reaching old age is a sign of the Most High's gracious benevolence. Longevity appears, therefore, as a special divine gift."

John Paul certainly used each day of his pontificate to the fullest. Author Gerard Mannion notes that "such longevity itself has consequences, not least the opportunity to model the Church according to one's own conception of what it should be." John Paul did just that. He understood well the Church's strengths and weaknesses, and he set a clear direction for the future — particularly in his implementation of the Second Vatican Council's initiatives (#9).

71 **Multilingual Communication.** John Paul II became fluent in at least eight languages — Polish, Italian, English, French, German, Spanish, Portuguese, and Latin. Some sources report that he was fluent in up to eleven. His father — who is now himself on the road to sainthood — was fluent in Polish and German, which he taught his sons at home. The future pope studied Slavic languages and Russian during his freshman year at Poland's Jagiellonian University. While studying in Rome for his doctorate, he had ample opportunity to study and practice Italian.

The polyglot pope was certainly able to communicate in (and read) dozens of languages. Much of this was thanks to his extensive travels before becoming pope. His linguistic talents allowed him the opportunity to connect with people around the world in a more direct and personal way, all for the sake of communicating Christ and the truths of the Faith.

A biographer writes that "when he knew a language, his knowledge was not ... merely phonetic, but also grammatical; he was familiar with its nuances. He was also familiar with the literature of other languages, since he liked to read in the original. In English, however, he had a pronounced Slavic accent and was less at ease, sometimes forced to grope for the right word when he was tired." According to the *Boston Globe,* John Paul's Spanish was weak when he became pope in 1978. However, he made learning that language a priority: by the time he visited Peru in 1985, the pope's knowledge of Spanish had improved dramatically.

John Paul annually offered greetings to the faithful around the world in up to sixty-five languages during his *Urbi et Orbi* address on Easter Sunday. Just a year before his death on April 2, 2005, he gave Easter greetings in sixty-two languages.

70 **His Productivity.** John Paul II's intellectual output was impressive not only because of the length of his pontificate but because he had honed an incredible work ethic early in his life. As archbishop of Kraków, he had a lamp and desk set up in his car so he could work while being driven to appointments. Wojtyła would typically rise at five thirty in the morning for prayer and Mass, followed by breakfast and a few hours for reading and writing. Biographer George Weigel writes:

> His energy may have seemed limitless to others, but he also paced himself well, never giving any task more time than it needed before moving on to the next. His ability to do two things at once — to run a seminar while working through his correspondence, for example — was another factor in his productivity. He also insisted on vacations, kayaking in the summer and skiing in the winter, which he believed were essential to recharging his stores of energy. But according to everyone who knew and worked with him, the mainspring of his daily energy was his constant prayer.

John Paul's father raised his sons to be self-disciplined in all aspects of their lives. The future pope followed a rigorous routine from the time he was a boy, rising early for prayer and breakfast before going to Mass and school. He also understood the value of hard work, which he described in his 1981 encyclical *Laborem Exercens* (On Human Work). The Holy Father contended that work makes a person "'more a human being.' ... Even when it is accompanied by toil and effort, work is still something good, and so man develops through love for work. This entirely *positive and creative, educational and meritorious character of man's work* must be the basis for the judgments and decisions being made today in its regard in spheres that include *human rights*."

John Paul wasn't technically the most prolific pope in history. He penned fourteen encyclicals (compared to Leo XIII's eighty-five), along with more than twenty apostolic exhortations and apostolic constitutions, forty-two apostolic letters, and three books. However, the depth and breadth of his writing, preaching, and teaching were enormous. His seminal Theology of the Body, for example, reset our understanding of the human person by establishing an anthropology in which the human body reveals God (#3). Given the depth and breadth of John Paul's teachings, there is little doubt his work will be unpacked and taught until the end of time. For this reason, he may well go down as the most productive pope in history.

69 **Prayer.** The intensity of John Paul II's prayer life — certainly among his most powerful and visible public witnesses to holiness — was a key factor in his effectiveness as pope. Because of this profound witness, throngs of the faithful pleaded *"Santo subito!"* ("Sainthood now!") immediately after his death.

Throughout his pontificate, he typically began his day at five thirty with at least an hour of solitary prayer in his private chapel. He would often lie prostrate in front of the tabernacle with his arms outstretched in a cruciform position. A portion of this intimate time before the Blessed Sacrament included intercession for those who sent him prayer requests, which the nuns from his household left in a drawer in his kneeler. He typically celebrated Mass at seven thirty in his private chapel with his secretaries, other bishops, and priests. This author was honored to attend three times. The small congregation (about thirty people) usually included invited guests and sometimes the nuns who cared for the papal apartment.

During his final visit to the United States in 1999, John Paul addressed young people, urging them to pray:

> You belong to Christ. … But you will get to know him truly and personally only through prayer. What is needed is that you talk to him, and listen to him. Today we are living in an age of instant communications. But do you realize what a unique form of communication prayer is? Prayer enables us to meet God at the most profound level of our being. It connects us directly to God: Father, Son and Holy Spirit, in a constant exchange of love. Through prayer you will learn to become the light of the world, because in prayer you become one with the source of our true light, Jesus himself.

68 **Education.** The cardinal archbishop of Kraków noticed young Father Wojtyła's exceptional giftedness and, in 1946, assigned him to further studies in Rome. At the Angelicum, he earned a licentiate of sacred theology in 1947 and successfully defended his doctoral thesis in philosophy, *The Doctrine of Faith in St. John of the Cross*, the following year.

He then returned to Poland to teach ethics at the Jagiellonian University. There, in 1954, he earned a doctorate in sacred theology. He subsequently taught at the Catholic University of Lublin, now renamed the John Paul II Catholic University of Lublin. While teaching, he gathered a small group of young people who began to call themselves *Rodzinka*, or "Little Family." They met for philosophical discussion, for prayer, and to help the sick. The group, which Wojtyła later called "my Środowisko," grew to nearly 200, and their activities expanded to include skiing and kayaking trips.

Clearly, education was of immense importance to John Paul. He stressed catechesis throughout his pontificate. In 1979, he praised faithful teachers: "The Church needs men and women who are intent on teaching by word and example — intent on helping to permeate the whole educational milieu with the spirit of Christ. ... Catholic education is above all a question of communicating Christ, of helping to form Christ in the lives of others." Twenty years later, he told youth in St. Louis that "your first responsibility is to get to know as much as you can about [Jesus], in your parishes, in religious instruction in your high schools and colleges, in your youth groups and Newman Centers." He also stressed that "the greatest contribution that authentically Catholic education can make to American culture is to restore ... the conviction that human beings can grasp the truth of things."

67 **Angels.** From the late 1980s through the '90s, angels were all the rage — particularly with the New Age movement. John Paul was ahead of the curve. In the summer of 1986, he delivered a series of talks he called "Catechesis on the Angels." These six lessons, delivered at his weekly general audience, drew on the Church's teachings on the nature of angels, their participation in salvation history, the rebellious angels, and Christ's victory over evil.

While New Age adherents refer to angels as "guides, entities, energies, and beings," John Paul clarified that they are "pure spirits, creatures of God, initially all good and then, through a choice of sin, irreducibly separated into angels of light and angels of darkness. And while the existence of the wicked angels requires of us that we be watchful so as not to yield to their empty promises, we are certain that the victorious power of Christ the Redeemer enfolds our lives, so that we ourselves may overcome these spirits. In this, we are powerfully helped by the good angels." He also emphasized that angels play a significant "part in the history of the salvation of man, in the moments established by divine Providence. ... This is believed and taught by the Church, on the basis of Sacred Scripture, from which we learn that the task of the good angels is the protection of people and solicitude for their salvation."

When John Paul visited the Italian Shrine of Saint Michael in 1987, he underscored the fact that spiritual warfare is real: "The battle against the devil, which is the principal task of Saint Michael the Archangel, is still being fought today, because the devil is still alive and active in the world."

66 **Teaching on Homosexuality.** The Church rarely expands its teaching on particular subjects until cultural change creates fertile ground for such development. For example, the Vatican didn't fully develop its position on contraception until the 1960s because until the twentieth century all Christian denominations fully accepted that artificially preventing conception was sinful.

Similarly, for a long time, there was little reason for the Church to plumb the depths of her teaching on the nature of homosexual behavior. In 1986, the Congregation for the Doctrine of the Faith issued a Letter to the Bishops of the Catholic Church on the Pastoral Care of Homosexual Persons. The letter explained the following: "Although the particular inclination of the homosexual person is not a sin, it is a more or less strong tendency ordered toward an intrinsic moral evil; and thus the inclination itself must be seen as an objective disorder. Therefore, special concern and pastoral attention should be directed toward those who have this condition, lest they be led to believe that the living out of this orientation in homosexual activity is a morally acceptable option. It is not."

The 1994 *Catechism*, issued under the order of John Paul II, taught that those with same-sex attraction must be "accepted with respect, compassion, and sensitivity. Every sign of unjust discrimination in their regard should be avoided. These persons are called … to unite to the sacrifice of the Lord's Cross the difficulties they may encounter from their condition" (CCC 2358).

The Holy Father went further in his 2005 book, *Memory and Identity*, blasting the European Union for recognizing homosexual unions and allowing same-sex couples to adopt children: "It is legitimate and necessary to ask oneself if this is not perhaps part of a new ideology of evil, perhaps more insidious and hidden, which attempts to pit human rights against the family and man."

65 **Christian Unity.** During Billy Graham's first meeting with John Paul II in 1981, the pope grabbed the American evangelist's thumb and said, "We are brothers." For the Holy Father, that was one of many victories in his efforts to bring the Body of Christ together. Throughout his pontificate, he met with dozens of faith leaders; his motivation to heal the divisions in Christianity was rooted in Jesus' prayer for unity in the Gospel of John (see Jn 17:21).

John Paul reaffirmed in 1985 that *"the Catholic Church is committed to the ecumenical movement with an irrevocable decision, and it desires to contribute to it with all its possibilities."* Ecumenism, he said, was one of his pastoral priorities: "This movement is aroused by the Holy Spirit and I consider myself deeply responsible for it." In 1986, after gathering world religious leaders in Assisi for the first World Day of Prayer for Peace, John Paul said that the event "can be considered as a visible illustration, a lesson of facts, a catechism intelligible to all, of what the ecumenical commitment and the commitment for interreligious dialogue presuppose and signify."

"The entire life of Christians is marked by a concern for ecumenism; and they are called to let themselves be shaped, as it were, by that concern," he wrote in *Ut Unum Sint* (On Commitment to Ecumenism), the first encyclical dedicated specifically to ecumenism. The 1995 document focused on healing divisions between the Catholic Church and other Christian communities — in particular Protestants and the Orthodox churches. George Weigel writes, "The first new thing about *Ut Unum Sint* was the unmistakable set of signals it sent throughout the Catholic Church. Those who thought ecumenism a Vatican II fad that would mercifully fade away were unquestionably informed that they were mistaken."

64 Outreach to the Orthodox Churches. John Paul II had a burning desire to develop a convivial relationship with the Catholic Church's separated Eastern brethren. Thirteen months into his term as pope, John Paul touched down in Turkey, meeting with Demetrios I, ecumenical patriarch of Constantinople. The visit led to Demetrios's reciprocal trip to Rome in 1987. Both men participated in Solemn Vespers at the Basilica of Saint Mary Major and Mass at Saint Peter's Basilica.

John Paul's trip to Romania in 1999 marked the first time a pope had visited a predominantly Eastern Orthodox country since the Great Schism of 1054, the event that separated Eastern Orthodoxy and Western Catholicism. Upon the pope's arrival, Romanian Orthodox Patriarch Teoctist stated: "The second millennium of Christian history began with a painful wounding of the unity of the Church; the end of this millennium has seen a real commitment to restoring Christian unity."

John Paul's 1995 encyclical *Ut Unum Sint* famously announced that "the Church must breathe with her two lungs!" — the Churches of the East and the West. The document also recalled John Paul's 1979 visit to Turkey, where he and Demetrios began "theological dialogue between the Catholic Church and all the Orthodox Churches in canonical communion with the See of Constantinople." That visit paved the way for the ecumenical patriarchate delegation's annual visit to Rome and the custom of a Holy See delegation visiting Istanbul.

Although his efforts at unity were imperfect, wrote one chronicler, "for John Paul II, the quest for Christian unity and the mutual exploration of truths that lead to the one Truth, who is God, are essential elements in the quest for a more humane world." Near the end of his papacy, John Paul said, "Christian unity has been a constant preoccupation of my Pontificate and continues to be a priority demand of my ministry."

63 **Diplomacy with Russia.** One of John Paul II's great-est disappointments was that he never had the occasion to visit Russia. The Russian government and the Holy See began discussing diplomatic relations in 1990, but it wasn't until 2009 that they officially established full diplomatic ties. In early 1998, Russian president Boris Yeltsin spent nearly an hour with the pope at the Vatican and repeated Mikhail Gorbachev's invita-tion for him to visit Russia. However, "absent an invitation from the Russian Orthodox Church and given the Pope's ecumenical commitments, no such pilgrimage was possible," wrote a biog-rapher.

The Russian Orthodox Church, the largest organization of Eastern Orthodoxy, had long accused the Catholic Church of proselytizing in Russia; property disputes also hampered efforts at unity. The Vatican, however, always maintained that it mere-ly serves existing Catholics in Russia, mainly those of Polish, German, and Lithuanian extraction. Because of long-standing tension between Russia and Poland, many Russian governmen-tal and religious leaders harbored distrust of the Polish pope. In 1997, John Paul and Patriarch Aleksy II had planned to meet and sign a joint declaration, but diplomatic missteps and other miscalculations led to the deal falling apart. Relations were fur-ther complicated by friction between the Holy See and the other Eastern Orthodox Churches.

However, in 2004, Cardinal Walter Kasper, then president of the Pontifical Council for Promoting Christian Unity, met with Aleksey in Moscow. Kasper called it "a first step" in the resumption of dialogue. Thanks to John Paul's groundbreaking diplomacy, tensions began to ease after Aleksey's death. His suc-cessor, Russian Orthodox Patriarch Kirill, met with Pope Fran-cis in 2016, a landmark step in healing the thousand-year-old rift between the Eastern and Western branches of Christianity.

62 **Visit to the United Kingdom.** After King Henry VIII broke with Rome in 1534, relations between Britain and the Holy See were rocky at best. The Catholic Emancipation Act of 1829 removed legal obstacles to relations with the Papal States, but Great Britain did not reestablish relations with the Holy See until 1914.

Queen Elizabeth II met privately with Pope Saint John XXIII at the Vatican in 1962. She made two official state visits during John Paul II's pontificate, one in 1980 and the other in 2000. The pope's diplomatic efforts were tested when, two months before his anticipated 1982 visit to the United Kingdom, war broke out in the Falkland Islands between England and Argentina. However, a month later, Sir Mark Heath presented his credentials to the pope, becoming Britain's first ambassador to the Holy See.

The 1982 visit was the first-ever papal journey to the United Kingdom. The six-day trip to England, Scotland, and Wales brought the pope to nine cities, where he delivered sixteen major addresses. He met with Queen Elizabeth and Prince Charles, and he held a joint service alongside the Anglican Archbishop of Canterbury at Canterbury Cathedral. During the service, the men renewed their baptismal vows, prayed at the spot where Saint Thomas Becket was murdered in 1170, and issued a declaration thanking God for "the progress that has been made in the work of reconciliation" between the two churches.

John Paul also addressed the General Assembly of the Church of Scotland and presided over five large, open-air Masses. More than two million people attended papal events — the biggest event for British Catholics since their emancipation. John Paul's efforts paved the way for Pope Benedict XVI in 2009 to establish ordinariates for Anglicans who wish to enter the Catholic Church.

61 **Speeches at the United Nations.** John Paul II was unafraid to speak truth to power. He had diplomatically worked around the communist rulers of Poland as a priest and bishop, and he had expertly navigated Church politics as a (mostly) behind-the-scenes influencer at the Second Vatican Council. His speeches at the United Nations — in 1979 and 1995 — challenged world leaders from a Christocentric worldview.

George Weigel writes, "On October 2, 1979, four weeks after he began his catechetical series on the Theology of the Body, John Paul II gave one of the crucial public addresses of his pontificate, to the General Assembly of the United Nations at its headquarters in New York. What he had to say about human rights was a direct challenge to the way most U.N. member states thought about international politics and the pursuit of peace." During the hour-long speech, he discussed human rights, leaning heavily on the importance of religious liberty: "It is a question of the highest importance that in internal social life, as well as in international life, *all human beings* in every nation and country *should be able to enjoy effectively their full rights under any political regime or system.*"

John Paul's 1995 address to the General Assembly noted the thirtieth anniversary of Paul VI's historic address to the General Assembly and the United Nations' fiftieth anniversary. He called nations to build a civilization of love: "Each and every human person has been created in the 'image and likeness' of the One who is the origin of all that is. We have within us the capabilities for wisdom and virtue. With these gifts, and with the help of God's grace, we can build in the next century and the next millennium a civilization worthy of the human person, a true culture of freedom. *We can and must do so!* And in doing so, we shall see that the tears of this century have prepared the ground for a new springtime of the human spirit."

60 **Inspiring Vocations.** In the challenging environment following the Second Vatican Council, religious vocations dropped sharply, but John Paul II inspired a generation to ponder God's call. There is a crop of clergy around the world today lovingly referred to as "John Paul II priests." He also inspired an untold number of holy marriages and single people committed to the Church.

The vocations crisis impacted Catholics worldwide. The world's bishops gathered for a synod in late 1990 to discuss priestly training. The result of that gathering was John Paul's 1992 document *Pastores Dabo Vobis* (On the Formation of Priests in the Circumstances of the Present Day). Like his predecessors, John Paul delivered an annual message in May for the World Day of Prayer for Vocations, and an annual message to priests on Holy Thursday. In each of these messages, he urged young men and women to plumb the depths of God in prayer, asking them to plead for holy vocations.

In his 2004 message regarding vocations, he said, "My heartfelt wish is that prayer for vocations be intensified ever more; prayer that is adoration of the mystery of God and thanksgiving for the *'great things'* that he has accomplished and does not cease to carry out." Regarding the priesthood, he said that same year, "In some places of the world the shortage of priests is all the more urgently felt since today the number of priests is dwindling without sufficient replacements from the younger generation. In other places, thank God, we see a promising spring-time of vocations. There is also a growing awareness among the People of God of the need to pray and work actively to promote vocations to the priesthood and to the consecrated life."

Certainly, John Paul's foresight in creating World Youth Day (#7) spurred many young hearts to embrace God's call to priesthood and religious life. Countries that have hosted the international gathering typically see a significant bump in vocations in subsequent years. According to Bishop Joseph Pepe, "This is very much an evangelical moment when it comes to considering the priesthood and religious life."

By his example of courage, John Paul also moved a generation of young men to embrace the priesthood. "He radiated a conviction, a confidence, a courage that a skeptical and frightened world craved," said Cardinal Timothy Dolan. "And young men were among them, reluctant to commit their lives to a question mark, but itching to embrace an exclamation point! They were tired of living in doubt and fear."

Knowing that the family is the seedbed for all vocations, John Paul also championed marriage and family life (#19): "A very special responsibility falls upon the Christian family, which by virtue of the sacrament of matrimony shares in its own unique way in the educational mission of the Church — teacher and mother."

59 **Intervening with the Jesuits.** Many popes have butted heads with the Society of Jesus since its formation in 1540, but few have so boldly confronted the order as did John Paul II in 1981. *Time* magazine reported on his actions: "In a move interpreted as a warning to all religious orders, he suspended the normal workings of the Jesuit Constitutions, removed the acting leader of the organization and replaced him with two Italian Jesuits who enjoy the Vatican's confidence."

In 1773, Pope Clement XIV dissolved the Jesuit order, and this dissolution lasted decades. In 1973, Paul VI demanded the order's obedience. Pope John Paul I had reportedly been preparing to reproach the Jesuits prior to his death in 1978; this was not lost on John Paul II when he assumed the Chair of Peter. Jesuit dissent during and in the aftermath of the Second Vatican Council had spiraled out of control as they took the council's liturgical changes rather liberally. One historian writes, "In Jesuit seminaries, for example, it became common for priests to celebrate Mass without vestments and with prayers and readings chosen or even composed by the students."

Two years before his intervention, John Paul II reprimanded the order's leadership for spreading confusion in the Church. Members of the Society had shocked the Vatican by challenging Church teaching on birth control, priestly celibacy, and the prohibition on female ordination. According to a 1982 *New York Times* article, "Other Church worries stem[med] from the sympathies of some Jesuits for guerrilla tactics in left-wing and pacifist causes. Jesuits [were] reportedly active in revolutionary movements in Guatemala and El Salvador."

John Paul's 1981 intervention had mixed results, turning some Jesuits into lifelong opponents of the Holy Father. According to one observer, "Others saw it as a chance to take stock of the ... years of experimentation and innovation."

58 **Defending Copernicus.** John Paul II had a kinship with Nicolaus Copernicus (1473–1543), the Renaissance-era mathematician and astronomer. Like Copernicus, John Paul was born in Poland and studied at Kraków's Jagiellonian University. The pope understood that the Church needed to set the record straight with regard to the esteemed scientist.

It was Copernicus's theory of heliocentrism (the sun as the center of the solar system) that got Galileo in trouble with the Church's Inquisition. The difference was that Copernicus only proposed it as a theory, whereas Galileo proclaimed it as a certainty. Since Scripture says, "You set the Earth on its foundations, so that it should never be shaken" (Ps 104:5), it was commonly believed that the rest of the universe revolved around the earth. Anyone who thought otherwise was considered a heretic.

The Church essentially banned Copernicus's book, *De Revolutionibus*, in 1616. By the end of the seventeenth century, however, the scientific community had largely accepted the heliocentric theory as fact. Pope Benedict XIV removed *De Revolutionibus* from the list of forbidden books in 1758, but it wasn't until Copernicus's fellow Pole became pope that the Catholic Church officially made amends and accepted his genius.

New Scientist quotes a 1993 letter John Paul wrote to organizers of an event marking the 450th anniversary of Copernicus's hypothesis: "Although Copernicus was not censured by the Church in his lifetime for his heretical idea, he was 'rejected by Catholic and Protestant theologians,' said the Pope. ... 'The claimed incompatibility between science and faith belongs to the past,' declared the Pope. He said Copernicus was not just a great scientist but also a great Catholic, who donated his medical services to the poor. His example, said the Pope, showed that great science is based on a 'spiritual force' able to inspire service 'to our brothers.'"

57 **Revisiting Galileo.** Today we take it for granted today that the sun is the center of our solar system. We have Galileo Galilei to thank for that. When the Italian astronomer and physicist discovered in 1610 that the earth was, contrary to popular opinion, *not* the center of the universe, the Catholic hierarchy was taken aback, as this fact seemed to contradict Sacred Scripture. The Inquisition denounced Galileo, first in 1616 and again in 1633, when the Church found him "vehemently suspect of heresy," condemning him to house arrest for the remainder of his life.

In 1979, John Paul II urged the Church to reexamine the circumstances of Galileo's conviction. In an address that year to the Pontifical Academy of Sciences, the pope acknowledged that the scientist had "suffered much … from men and Church organizations." Two years later, writes his biographer, the pope established "a commission to reexamine the entire Galileo case, which had become a powerful cultural myth underwriting hostile secularism's conviction that biblical religion and science were simply incompatible."

The commission's report, issued in 1992 by the Pontifical Council for Culture, acknowledged that the Church tribunal judging Galileo's scientific positions contained significant errors. John Paul then expressed regret for how the Inquisition handled the Galileo case in another address to the Pontifical Academy of Sciences: "From the Galileo affair we can learn a lesson which remains valid in relation to similar situations which occur today and which may occur in the future. … [O]ften beyond two partial contrasting perceptions, there exists a wider perception which includes them and goes beyond both of them. … The error of the theologians of the time … was to think that our understanding of the physical world's structure was, in some way, imposed by the literal sense of Sacred Scripture."

56 **Faith and Science.** The Church's errors in the Galileo affair and other such incidents led many to pronounce that faith and science were irreconcilable. John Paul II worked vigorously to erase any doubt that Christianity and science are necessary for each other's good. He wrote that "science can purify religion from error and superstition; religion can purify science from idolatry and false absolutes. Each can draw the other into a wider world, a world in which both can flourish."

The pope began his outreach early in his pontificate. In 1979, he called on scholars, historians, and theologians to "dispel the mistrust that still opposes, in many minds, a fruitful concord between science and faith, between the Church and the world. To this task that will honor the truth of faith and science, and to open the door to future collaborations, I assure all my support."

The Holy Father convened an international research conference in 1987 to begin a new level of dialogue and mutual understanding among scientists, philosophers, and theologians. The event helped bridge a centuries-old gap between the Church and the academy. He raised some eyebrows when, in a 1996 address to the Pontifical Academy of Sciences, he said that "new knowledge has led to the recognition of more than one hypothesis in the theory of evolution."

Later in his pontificate, in a 2000 address to the Pontifical Academy, he pronounced that "science shines forth in all its value as a good capable of motivating an existence, as a great experience of freedom for truth, as a fundamental work of service. Through it, each researcher feels that he is able himself to grow, and to help others to grow, in humanity."

55 **Anticipating Climate Change.** The term "climate change" wasn't popularized until well after John Paul II's death in 2005, but concern for creation and environmental damage caused by humans was on the Holy Father's mind throughout his pontificate. The pope taught a whole-earth approach to ecology. "The earth will not continue to offer its harvest, except with *faithful stewardship*," he told American farmworkers in 1987. "We cannot say we love the land and then take steps to destroy it for use by future generations."

At times, John Paul sounded quite pessimistic about man's ability to take care of the earth. "If we scan the regions of our planet, we immediately see that humanity has disappointed God's expectations. Man, especially in our time, has without hesitation devastated wooded plains and valleys, polluted waters, disfigured the earth's habitat, made the air unbreathable." He recognized that pollution, which reached its zenith in the West during the 1970s and '80s, is an issue the industrialized world needs to contend with.

"Faced with the widespread destruction of the environment, people everywhere are coming to understand that we cannot continue to use the goods of the earth as we have in the past," he said in his 1990 World Day of Peace message. "A new *ecological awareness* is beginning to emerge which, rather than being downplayed, ought to be encouraged to develop into concrete programmes and initiatives." He lamented that "world peace is threatened not only by the arms race, regional conflicts and continued injustices among peoples and nations, but also by a lack of *due respect for nature*, by the plundering of natural resources and by a progressive decline in the quality of life. The sense of precariousness and insecurity that such a situation engenders is a seedbed for collective selfishness, disregard for others and dishonesty."

54 **Defense of Agriculture.** While the saintly pope made clear his concern for the planet, he also had a keen appreciation for those who till the earth and produce food for humanity. "The world of agriculture, which provides society with the goods it needs for its daily sustenance, is of *fundamental importance*," he wrote.

During his first visit to the United States in 1979, he made the unusual choice of visiting Living History Farms on the outskirts of Des Moines, Iowa, after receiving a handwritten letter from Iowa farmer Joe Hayes. The event drew the largest crowd in the state's history — a whopping 350,000 pilgrims. "To all of you who are farmers and all who are associated with agricultural production, I want to say this: The Church highly esteems your work," he said. "You support the lives of millions who themselves do not work on the land, but who live because of what you produce. ... Farmers everywhere provide bread for all humanity, but it is Christ alone who is the bread of life."

During the Great Jubilee, the Holy Father reminded the world that access to food is the right of every human being, calling poverty and hunger "an intolerable scandal. ... *We can no longer limit ourselves to academic reflections*: we must rid humanity of this disgrace through appropriate political and economic decisions with a global scope." He called for sustainable agriculture, noting that the earth is for man's "*use*, not *abuse*." He warned that agricultural advances "through the application of biotechnologies ... cannot be evaluated solely on the basis of immediate economic interests. They must be submitted beforehand to rigorous scientific and ethical examination, to prevent them from becoming disastrous for human health and the future of the earth."

53 **Guiding Economic Policy.** Business, labor, and industry must all be at the service of the common good, John Paul II taught in his vast body of work on economics. He was particularly concerned for workers and the poor. While he rejected Marxism out of hand, the pope was a regular critic of greed-is-good, "unbridled capitalism."

John Paul believed that it is the Church's place to guide rather than to create economic policy: "The Church does not propose economic and political systems or programs, nor does she show preference for one or the other, provided that human dignity is properly respected and promoted, and provided she herself is allowed the room she needs to exercise her ministry in the world."

His teaching delved into the dignity of work, just wages, and how the economy must benefit all without exploitation of workers. He wrote that "the poor ask for the right to share in enjoying material goods and to make good use of their capacity for work, thus creating a world that is more just and prosperous for all. The advancement of the poor constitutes a great opportunity for the moral, cultural and even economic growth of all humanity." In step with his predecessors — particularly Leo XIII, whose 1891 encyclical *Rerum Novarum* pioneered Catholic teaching with regard to economics and work — John Paul bolstered workers' right to form unions and to strike.

As one writer expressed it in *The New York Times*: "Ultimately, John Paul's economic thinking [came] down to faith and hope. He deeply [believed] humanity is capable of moral enlightenment and he [was] convinced that spiritual awakening is the one sure answer to social injustice. By this measure, the key to his success [lay] not in the weight of his ideas but in his success as a pastor."

52 **Addressing Poverty.** Even before he became pope, Wojtyła was a tireless champion of the poor. He spent four years as an impoverished laborer during the German Nazi occupation of Poland, learning lessons he would turn into teachings that would change the world. As a priest, bishop, and pope, he stood with Poland's poor and vulnerable — at Nowa Huta and with the Solidarity movement.

In dozens of documents and addresses, John Paul said more about economic matters than any of his predecessors. He addressed poverty during his first U.S. visit: "You must never be content to leave [the poor] just the crumbs from the feast. You must take of your substance, and not just of your abundance, in order to help them. And you must treat them like guests at your family table." He argued for both economic development and a preferential option for the poor. "One of the greatest injustices in the contemporary world consists precisely in this: that the ones who possess much are relatively few and those who possess almost nothing are many. It is the injustice of the poor distribution of the goods and services originally intended for all."

At the close of the Great Jubilee, he again drew attention to poverty: "Our world is entering the new millennium burdened by the contradictions of an economic, cultural and technological progress which offers immense possibilities to a fortunate few, while leaving millions of others not only on the margins of progress but in living conditions far below the minimum demanded by human dignity. How can it be that even today there are still people dying of hunger? Condemned to illiteracy? Lacking the most basic medical care? Without a roof over their heads? ... Christians must learn to make their act of faith in Christ by discerning His voice in the cry for help that rises from this world of poverty."

51 **Visit to Cuba.** When John Paul II traveled, he created history, and his 1998 visit to Cuba was no exception. The island nation had lived under the iron fist of Fidel Castro's communist government for nearly forty years, and the pope hoped to spur change. *"May Cuba, with all its magnificent potential, open itself up to the world, and may the world open itself up to Cuba,"* he said upon his arrival.

He called for an end to America's long-standing trade sanctions, calling the policy "oppressive, unjust and ethically unacceptable." He also pressed Castro to allow greater religious freedom. He condemned abortion (at the time there were sixty abortions for every one hundred live births in Cuba) and sexual promiscuity, and he called for parents to take a greater role in their children's lives.

As he had done in Poland (#30), John Paul advocated for spiritual renewal that would bring greater freedom for all Cubans. During his five-day apostolic journey to the island country, he did not mention the Castro regime or the revolution. As George Weigel writes, "He had come to give back to the people of Cuba their authentic history and culture. There was no need to make reference to the men who had reduced their island to penury. That was the past; that was an aberration. He had come to tell the truth about the past and present, to spark hope for the future, and to inspire Cubans to be the protagonists of their destiny."

The visit led to a thaw in U.S.-Cuba relations. Relations between Cuba and the United States were formally reestablished in 2015, with the opening of the Cuban embassy in Washington and the U.S. embassy in Havana. The regime allowed the Church more freedom than she had known in decades. One small victory was that Castro allowed the public celebration of Christmas for the first time in 1998 (initially for one year only). However, it has remained a public holiday ever since.

50 **"Be Not Afraid!"** From his first Mass as pope to the last days of his life, John Paul II repeated many times what became a primary theme of his pontificate: "Be not afraid!" (His motto, of course, was *"Totus Tuus"* [#10].) At the heart of this call was the truth that people — Christians and non-Christians alike — should not fear to open their hearts completely to Jesus Christ, allowing him to transform them from within.

"Help the pope and all those who wish to serve Christ and with Christ's power to serve the human person and the whole of mankind," he said at his inaugural Mass in 1978. "Do not be afraid. Open wide the doors for Christ. To his saving power open the boundaries of States, economic and political systems, the vast fields of culture, civilization and development. Do not be afraid. Christ knows 'what is in man.' He alone knows it."

John Paul was especially persuasive with youth, calling young people to be bold in their faith. He had repeatedly addressed this same theme to young people from the time he was a priest in Poland, gathering his *Rodzinka*, or "Little Family." When he addressed World Youth Day pilgrims in 1993, he charged them to be evangelists in their own day and age. "Do not be afraid to go out on the streets and into public places, like the first apostles who preached Christ and the Good News of salvation in the squares of cities, towns and villages. This is no time to be ashamed of the Gospel." In 1999, he encouraged European youth to strive for holiness: "Do not be afraid to be holy," he said. "Do not be satisfied with mediocrity. The kingdom of heaven is for those who are determined to enter it."

John Paul explained in his 1994 book *Crossing the Threshold of Hope* that he pleaded with mankind to "be not afraid" in order to convince us to trust Jesus completely:

> When, on October 22, 1978, I said the words "Be not afraid!" in St. Peter's Square, I could not fully know how far they would take me and the entire Church. Their meaning came more from the Holy Spirit, the Consoler

promised by the Lord Jesus to His disciples, than from the man who spoke them. Nevertheless, with the passing of the years, I have recalled these words on many occasions. ... *Why should we have no fear? Because* man has been redeemed by God. ... *The power of Christ's Cross and Resurrection is greater than any evil which man could or should fear.*

49 **Relations with the Middle East.** When John Paul II was elected pope in 1978, the Middle East was a powder keg, ready to explode at any moment. Sadly, not much has changed since. Paul VI had been the first successor of Peter in modern times to visit the Holy Land, stopping in Israel and Jordan in 1964. During his pontificate, John Paul visited several Middle Eastern countries, including Jordan, Israel, Syria, Lebanon, and Egypt. He understood that there were no easy answers to peace in the region, which has known nothing but conflict for centuries.

However, he made some concrete moves toward stability in the region by establishing diplomatic relations between the Holy See and the State of Israel in 1993 (#48); establishing official relations with the Palestinian Authority in 1994; convening a special assembly of the Synod of Bishops for Lebanon, which resulted in a papal visit to Lebanon in 1997; and opposing the 1991 and 2003 United States–led wars against Iraq. During the First Gulf War, the pope convened a special gathering of bishops — including seven patriarchs — from all countries involved in the conflict, plus delegates from Europe, North Africa, and the United States.

George Weigel writes that John Paul believed that "the Church's mission in world politics was to teach the relevant moral principles that ought to guide international statecraft. Beyond that, it was the responsibility of statesmen to make prudential judgments on the question of when nonviolent means of resolving a conflict and restoring order had been exhausted."

Building on John Paul II's efforts at diplomacy, the Holy See continues to strive diligently for peace and security in the Middle East. His legacy continues through top-level discussions with Israel and Palestine regarding peace in the region, freedom of conscience, religious liberty, and protection of holy sites.

48 Visit to Israel. As a young lad in Wadowice, Poland, Wojtyła (nicknamed "Lolek") passed the time by playing soccer — usually as goalie — on a team made up primarily of Jewish boys. Having grown up during the Holocaust, in the midst of some of the greatest atrocities the world has ever seen, young Wojtyła had a heart for the Jewish people. As pope, he also had a fondness for Israel.

John Paul established diplomatic relations between the Holy See and Israel in 1993 after the two states approved a Fundamental Accord. "Jewish-Christian relations," he said, "are never an academic exercise. They are, on the contrary, part of the very fabric of our religious commitments and our respective vocations as Christians and as Jews."

During the Great Jubilee, he made his one and only papal visit to Israel. (He had gone on pilgrimage to the Holy Land in 1963, shortly before being named archbishop of Kraków.) During the 2000 visit, he prayed at Jerusalem's Western Wall, leaving a written prayer expressing sorrow for Jews' suffering at the hands of Christians. The most touching moment of the pilgrimage was his address at Yad Vashem, the Holocaust memorial in Jerusalem. He said, "I assure the Jewish people that the Catholic Church, motivated by the Gospel law of truth and love and by no political considerations, is deeply saddened by the hatred, acts of persecution and displays of anti-Semitism directed against the Jews by Christians at any time and in any place."

In 1991, Cristina Odone, then editor of the *Catholic Herald*, described John Paul's long-standing passion "to place his Church at the heart of a new religious alliance that would bring together Jews, Muslims and Christians in a great armada of God's troops on earth."

47 **Visits to Africa.** Paul VI was the first pope in modern history to visit Africa, but John Paul II paid sustained attention to the continent during the last two decades of his pontificate. Over the course of his long reign, he made fourteen trips to Africa, visiting almost every country on the continent. His presence, teaching, and passion for its people had a powerful impact on Africa's political, economic, and social life.

The pope canonized dozens of African saints and created more than a dozen African cardinals. He appointed bishops from the continent, including Cardinal Francis Arinze and Cardinal Bernardin Gantin, to some of the most powerful positions in the Church. John Paul also convened a Synod of Bishops for Africa in 1994 that placed the continent at the center of the universal Church. In his post-synodal document *Ecclesia in Africa*, he "provided a road-map pointing to a greater role for the Church in using the Gospel to bring succor to a troubled continent."

Although Catholics outside of Africa were largely unaware of the apostolic exhortation, on the continent it became the basis for a productive conversation between bishops and their people — particularly in the aftermath of apartheid in South Africa, the famine that gripped the continent during the early 1980s, and the horrific genocide in Rwanda in 1994.

"Africans have a profound religious sense, a sense of the sacred, of the existence of God the Creator and of a spiritual world," John Paul wrote in *Ecclesia in Africa*, which he issued in person during an apostolic visit to Yaoundé, the capital of Cameroon. "The reality of sin in its individual and social forms is very much present in the consciousness of these peoples, as is also the need for rites of purification and expiation."

46 **Love of Italy.** On the evening of October 16, 1978, when Cardinal Wojtyła stepped out onto the loggia of Saint Peter's Basilica for the first time as Pope John Paul II, he addressed the excited throng in perfect Italian. Some were confused, because they understood from the introduction that he was not an Italian. Of course, Wojtyła had visited Italy many times as a priest and bishop, and he had lived in Rome while studying at the Angelicum during the 1940s.

In his unscripted remarks, the new pope said, "I don't know if I can explain myself well in your — in *our* — Italian language. If I make a mistake, you will correct me." In that moment, the Polish pope charmed the Italians and forever won their hearts. It was appropriate (and necessary) that he do so, since he was the first non-Italian pope since Adrian VI (1522–1523), a Dutchman. The normally fickle Italian public had fully embraced him as their own pope: "'At last,' [exulted] one local cleric, 'we have a Bishop of Rome!'"

In the first month of his pontificate, John Paul addressed Italian youth. He spoke of his affection for them and called them "to seek, love and bear witness to Jesus! This is your commitment; these are the instructions I leave you! By doing so, not only will you keep real joy in your lives, but also you will benefit the whole of society, which needs, above all, consistency with the evangelical message."

Over the course of his twenty-six-year pontificate, John Paul crisscrossed Italy dozens of times, and he visited all but a few of the Catholic churches in the diocese of Rome. He stirred an outpouring of affection in the hearts of the Italian people exceeding that of any pope in modern history, other than perhaps Pope Saint John XXIII.

45 **Affirming Natural Law.** As with other subjects he tackled, John Paul II approached law based on a sound anthropology. His guidance for those in the legal profession was based on a thorough understanding of the human person and our relationship with God. He knew that because the law is a great teacher of right and wrong, it has a profound impact on culture, politics, and human freedom. As law professor John Coverdale put it: "For John Paul II, the law is not an isolated technical discipline unmoored from a larger system of morality. Rather, it is an instrument in our search for the human fulfillment that is the goal of morality. As such, it necessarily reflects a set of moral aspirations."

The pope always discussed "natural law" in the context of the law that God has written on every human heart. "Human law should reflect and safeguard the natural and divine law, that is always a freeing truth," he said in 2002. He also affirmed in *Evangelium Vitae* that the law must guarantee the natural rights of everyone, particularly the most vulnerable: "Civil law must ensure that all members of society enjoy respect for certain fundamental rights which innately belong to the person, rights which every positive law must recognize and guarantee. First and fundamental among these is the inviolable right to life of every innocent human being."

Coverdale further writes that "John Paul II offers a penetrating and remarkably coherent set of answers to the most fundamental questions lawyers face as persons, as professionals, and as citizens. [He gives a] vigorous defense of the dignity and value of every human life and his stress on the role of interpersonal relations in the development of each individual marks out a path between the two extremes which mar contemporary understandings of the human condition."

44 **Consecrated Women.** John Paul II had profound respect for women, particularly for consecrated women. However, that fondness was tested from the get-go, just one year into his papacy.

During the pope's 1979 visit to Washington, D.C., he was to address women religious at the National Shrine of the Immaculate Conception. In her welcoming remarks, the head of the Leadership Conference of Women Religious, Sister Theresa Kane, respectfully challenged the Supreme Pontiff to open "all ministries of the Church to women." She was also among a group of about fifty women religious at the gathering who stood in silence to protest the pope's remarks. Not acknowledging the protest, the pope began his prepared address: "I am happy for this occasion because of my esteem for religious life, and my gratitude to women religious for their invaluable contribution to the mission and very life of the Church."

John Paul ended the debate on women's ordination with his 1994 apostolic letter *Ordinatio Sacerdotalis*: "I declare that the Church has no authority whatsoever to confer priestly ordination on women and that this judgment is to be definitively held by all the Church's faithful." Later that year, after the World Synod of Bishops deliberated on the consecrated life, the pope took the opportunity to stress fidelity. "I join the Fathers of the Synod in strongly recommending to men and women religious that they wear their proper habit," John Paul said in his 1996 post-synodal exhortation *Vita Consecrata*. "In the consecrated life, particular importance attaches to the spousal meaning," he wrote. "This spousal dimension, which is part of all consecrated life, has a particular meaning for women, who find therein their feminine identity and as it were discover the special genius of their relationship with the Lord."

43 **Elevation of Women.** In an effort to counter the wrongful vilification of the Catholic Church as being "anti-woman," John Paul II went out of his way to elevate women, while at the same time holding fast to two thousand years of Catholic teaching.

Although the sexual revolution officially began around 1964, Wojtyła was ahead of the curve when he published *Love and Responsibility* in 1960 as an antidote to the growing relaxation of sexual norms. The book upheld the dignity of women by teaching that spouses are meant as gifts to each other. As pope, John Paul developed his teaching on the dignity of women in his Theology of the Body (#3). His profound respect for women was expressed in his devotion to Our Lady, reflected in his apostolic motto, *Totus Tuus* (#10). However, he went further with two profound, groundbreaking documents: his 1988 apostolic letter *Mulieris Dignitatem* and his 1995 Letter to Women.

He wrote *Mulieris Dignitatem* (On the Dignity and Vocation of Women) to mark what is traditionally held to be the two thousandth anniversary of Our Lady's birth. Importantly, he coined the phrase "feminine genius" to describe traits and gifts that are unique to women: "The Church gives thanks *for all the manifestations of the feminine 'genius'* which have appeared in the course of history, in the midst of all peoples and nations."

His 1995 Letter to Women honored females of every stripe — mothers, wives, sisters, daughters, workers, and consecrated women. He wrote, "Transcending the established norms of his own culture, Jesus treated women with openness, respect, acceptance and tenderness. In this way he honoured the dignity which women have always possessed according to God's plan and in his love."

42 **Teaching on Sports.** It's no secret that John Paul II was an athlete. He played soccer as a child in Poland, enjoyed hiking and kayaking with young people as a young priest, and even sneaked past the Swiss Guard more than a hundred times over the course of his papacy to go hiking and skiing with his inner circle of priests.

He drew heavily on Saint Paul, himself an athlete, to convey the truths of the Faith. Addressing youth in St. Louis during his final US visit in 1999, the pope said, "Today, this impressive stadium has become another kind of training ground — not for hockey or soccer or basketball, but for that training that will help you to live your faith in Jesus more decisively. This is the 'training in devotion' that Saint Paul is referring to — the training that makes it possible for you to give yourselves without reservation to the Lord and to the work that he calls you to do!"

John Paul taught that sports can be a school of true human virtue. *"Playing sports has become very important today,* since it can encourage young people to develop important values such as loyalty, perseverance, friendship, sharing and solidarity," he told athletes during a Jubilee of Sports Mass in 2000. "Sports, in fact, can make an effective contribution to peaceful understanding between peoples and to establishing the new civilization of love."

In his Angelus address on January 1, 2000, John Paul spoke to those running the Rome Marathon: "Life can be compared to a unique marathon which we are all called to run, each in his own way and at his own pace. A common goal awaits us, however, and it is the encounter with Christ."

41 **The Mystery of Suffering.** The problem of pain is one that believers and nonbelievers have struggled with since the fall of Adam. John Paul II lived out this mystery in real time, especially during the last few years of his life. "The Holy Father's illness and suffering ... was one long martyrdom from start to finish," according to his longtime personal secretary, Cardinal Stanisław Dziwisz. "Karol Wojtyła had learned to accept suffering as a part of human existence and thus to live with pain and sickness." Dziwisz acknowledged that the pope was able to accept this cross because of his intense prayer life and love for Christ.

But John Paul was well acquainted with suffering long before his health deteriorated. Perhaps most poignantly, he lost both parents and his brother during his youth — between 1929 and 1941. During his 1998 visit to Cuba, he explored suffering: *"Pain is a mystery, often inscrutable to reason. It forms part of the mystery of the human person,* which alone comes clear in Jesus Christ who reveals to man man's true identity. Christ alone enables us to know the meaning of all that is human."

In his magnificent apostolic letter on redemptive suffering, *Salvifici Doloris,* he wrote that in a person who suffers, "God has confirmed his desire to act especially through suffering, which is man's weakness and emptying of self, and he wishes to make his power known precisely in this weakness and emptying of self." Most importantly, he wrote, suffering presents an opportunity for compassion — to open our hearts to those in pain, to be channels of God's grace, *"to unleash love in the human person,* that unselfish gift of one's 'I' on behalf of other people, especially those who suffer."

40 **Response to the sexual abuse crisis.** The abuse of minors by priests worldwide during the middle of the twentieth century is one of the most painful chapters in the Catholic Church's two-thousand-year history. Despite the fact that the abuse of minors has been shown to correlate strongly with the increase of homosexual men in the priesthood from the 1950s through the 1980s, the crisis did not explode publicly in the United States until 2002, at a time when John Paul II was plagued by health issues.

Critics accuse the pope of not doing enough to stop predatory priests and for being sluggish in responding to the crisis. However, former papal spokesman Joaquin Navarro-Valls told reporters that in 2002 very few — including John Paul — understood the depth and breadth of the situation.

In 1994, at the request of U.S. bishops seeking to implement a zero-tolerance policy, John Paul approved changes to Church law to allow the proposed norms, and two years later did the same for Irish bishops. The pope also made it obligatory for Church officials to report each case of priestly abuse directly to the Vatican's Congregation for the Doctrine of the Faith.

When he addressed American bishops in 2002, he made it clear that the Church would have no tolerance for abuse of minors. "People need to know that there is no place in the priesthood and religious life for those who would harm the young," he said. "They must know that bishops and priests are totally committed to the fullness of Catholic truth on matters of sexual morality, a truth as essential to the renewal of the priesthood and the episcopate as it is to the renewal of marriage and family life." The pope was also blunt in expressing his horror at the scandal, which cast a great deal of mistrust upon the Church and the priests entrusted with bringing Jesus to the world. "Like you, I too have been deeply grieved by the fact that priests and religious, whose vocation it is to help people live holy lives in the sight of God, have themselves caused such suffering and scandal to the young. ... The abuse which has caused this crisis is by every standard wrong and rightly considered a crime by society; it is also an appalling sin in the eyes of God." At the same time, the pope expressed solidarity with the abused. "To the victims and their families, wherever they may be, I express my profound sense of solidarity and concern," he said.

Chicago's Cardinal Francis George said the 2002 meeting with John Paul affirmed that homosexuality among priests was a pressing concern. "A definite connection was made between homosexuality and sexual misconduct with minors if the conduct is with minor men," George said. "If you have a man who cannot see himself as a married man with children, I don't think he has a vocation to the priesthood."

Papal biographer George Weigel pushed back on the idea that the pope ignored the crisis. "I think the only way to think about that comprehensibly is to understand that John Paul II was a great reformer of the Catholic priesthood," he said. "The Catholic priesthood in 1978 was in the worst condition it had been in since the sixteenth century. Thousands of priests had left the active ministry. We now know that a small minority of priests were involved in horrible crimes and grave sins. Seminary formation was weak. All of that was changed over the next twenty six and a half years."

39 **Outreach to Children.** Much to the chagrin of his security detail, John Paul II had a penchant for kissing babies during his weekly general audience in Saint Peter's Square and on foreign trips, where he would take them on his lap or stroke their cheeks. His tenderness for children derived from his admiration for their innocence and purity. As a young priest, he gathered a community of young people around him and soon earned the nickname "*Wujek*," or "Uncle."

As pope, John Paul frequently touched on the lessons that children can teach us. In 1994, he penned a Letter to Children — the very first papal document written specifically for children. He wrote, "*The Pope counts very much on your prayers. We must pray together and pray hard, that humanity, made up of billions of human beings, may become more and more the family of God and able to live in peace. … You instinctively turn away from hatred and are attracted by love: for this reason, the Pope is certain that you will not refuse his request.*"

A year later, on the World Day of Peace, he focused the spotlight on children's suffering as victims of abuse, war, violence, and neglect. The answer, he said, can be found in Jesus Christ, who welcomed little children. "A peaceful childhood will enable boys and girls to face the future with confidence. Let no one stifle their joyful enthusiasm and hope," he said.

As the Great Jubilee was drawing to a close, the Holy Father again welcomed children. More than six thousand gathered in Rome; millions around the world watched on television. "Dear young people, keep aloft and shining brightly the lamp of faith," he told them. "With this light, illumine the paths of life; set the world ablaze with love!"

38 **Love of the Circus.** John Paul II had a flair for the dramatic and a passion for peace. So in his first general audience after the 1981 attempt on his life, he invited a Moscow-based circus troupe — complete with Mashka, a dancing bear — to perform for him in Saint Peter's Square. According to a former Swiss Guard, the pope vowed that "there would be no talk of politics or war at the audience (this was not long after Soviet troops invaded Afghanistan). This was, he promised the Soviets, an event intended to celebrate life and friendship among people, nothing more."

John Paul established the Pontifical Council for the Pastoral Care of Migrants and Itinerant People in 1988, with a special section dedicated to circus workers. In keeping with the tradition set by his predecessors, he welcomed circus performers to the Vatican multiple times.

In 1993, international representatives of circus ministries presented the pontiff with a Ringling Brothers jacket embroidered with his name. "Under the form of entertainment, you demonstrate true human virtues," he told those gathered for that year's international meeting on the pastoral care of circus workers. The pope praised the performers for exemplifying the "qualities of patience, courage, sense of measured risk and collective play." He also noted that spectators could learn valuable lessons from the teamwork of circus people, who are "at peace with their own bodies and also with animals."

In 2004, the Holy Father addressed the Seventh International Congress for the Pastoral Care of Circus and Travelling Show People. He told participants that the circus and amusement parks "can also serve to spearhead the great themes of pastoral care, ecumenism and meetings between members of other religions and the common commitment to build up a universal brotherhood."

37 **Response to Medjugorje.** When reports surfaced in 1981 that the Blessed Mother was appearing to children in a village in what is now Bosnia-Herzegovina, the world was captivated. Six months later, the local bishop, Pavao Žanić, established a commission to investigate.

The bishop, who initially supported the visionaries, who were backed by the local Franciscan priests, issued his commission's report in 1986, ruling that the events at Medjugorje were *Non constat de supernaturalitate* — that is, neither approved nor condemned, but further study is needed to determine whether a supernatural character is present. Subsequent commissions held to those findings — including a thus far definitive ruling in 1991 by the Yugoslavia Bishops' Conference.

In 1996, a top official from the Vatican's Congregation for the Doctrine of the Faith stated that diocesan and parish pilgrimages to Medjugorje were prohibited. John Paul did not speak or write publicly about the alleged apparitions. According to an *Inside the Vatican* article, "In a meeting with Bishop Paul Hnilica, the Pope reportedly said: 'If I were not the Pope, I would probably have visited Medjugorje by now.' During a meeting with the Superior General of the Franciscan Order, the Holy Father asked: 'All around Medjugorje bombs have been falling, and yet Medjugorje itself was never damaged. Is this not perhaps a miracle of God?'"

Cardinal Dziwisz disputes that John Paul made those comments. Out of prudence, he said, the pope did not receive the "visionaries" in an audience. However, he noted that "the Holy Father was deeply impressed by the abundant spiritual fruits Medjugorje was able to unleash." It is notable that John Paul did not mention Medjugorje — or pay a visit — during his 1997 trip to Sarajevo, a mere ninety-five miles from the village.

36 **Our Lady of Częstochowa.** For those not familiar with the Polish language, the word *Częstochowa* (pronounced ches-stah-hoh-vah) is a mouthful. However, most Catholics know Our Lady of Częstochowa as the "Black Madonna," a venerated icon of the Blessed Mother housed at the Jasna Góra Monastery in Częstochowa, Poland. Legend holds that Saint Luke painted the image on the Holy Family's cedar table.

John Paul II's heart was drawn to Our Lady (#10) because of her profound love for Jesus, so this devotion came to him naturally. It was at the Jasna Góra shrine that a young Karol Wojtyła grew in his devotion to Mary after the heartbreak of being orphaned shortly before his twenty-first birthday. During his triumphant 1979 visit to Poland (#30), he called the monastery "a shrine of great hope," where "so many times I had whispered *Totus tuus* in prayer" before the image.

During that visit, which included a Mass that drew a million of his countrymen, the pope recounted that Poland had been entrusted to Our Lady many times throughout history. He again consecrated his native land and the entire Church to her protection: "*I entrust to you, Mother of the Church, all the problems of this Church, the whole of her mission and of her service, while the second millennium of the history of Christianity on earth is about to draw to a close.*"

He visited Częstochowa several times, including in 1991, when he again drew a million people to the shrine during the third international World Youth Day (#7). He was so devoted to the Black Madonna image that he kept an icon of her at the foot of the cross in his private chapel in the papal apartments.

35 **Care for the Swiss Guard.** Anyone who has visited the Vatican knows that the Swiss Guard have an unmistakable presence there. Established in 1506, the Pontifical Swiss Guard is among the world's oldest military units in continuous operation. Following the failed attempt on John Paul II's life in 1981, the Guard beefed up its nonceremonial roles and enhanced its training in unarmed combat and small arms.

John Paul regularly celebrated Mass for the Swiss Guard during their annual swearing-in ceremony. He had tremendous admiration for the force and habitually showed a paternal affection for the men charged with protecting him. He told them, "It is also important that you use your stay in Rome as a unique chance to sharpen your image as Christians. I am thinking especially of your spiritual life: you must ask yourselves what God's plan is for each of you. At the same time, I call your attention to how important brotherly relations are between those who call themselves Christian, both on and off duty."

Andreas Widmer, a former Swiss Guard, spent his first Christmas away from home in 1986. When the pope emerged from his apartment to celebrate midnight Christmas Mass, he saw a sullen-looking Widmer at his post. "This is your first Christmas away from home, isn't it?" the pope asked. "Yes, Your Holiness," he replied. The pope responded, "I will pray for you at Mass this evening." "That was all I needed," Widmer writes. "Someone had noticed my pain. Someone had cared, and that someone was the pope himself. In that moment, I felt comforted. Now, looking back, I feel amazed. Here was the leader of a billion Catholics ... yet he was still sensitive enough to perceive the emotions of a twenty-year-old guard whose sole job was to blend into the background as he passed."

34 **Care for the Police.** Before flying out of Newark Airport in 1995, John Paul II took several minutes to spend time with police officers from the New York metro area who had helped to ensure his safety during his four-day visit. He chatted with the officers, kissed their little children, and even wrote a message in an officer's Bible.

John Paul understood well that his worldwide effort to evangelize hinged on security forces' performing their duties effectively at the Vatican and around the world. In several addresses to law enforcement in Italy, the Vatican, and Great Britain, the pope lauded those who serve and protect. "Persevere in your commitment to the service of justice," he told the Carabinieri, the Italian national police force, in 1988. "It is with the power of justice, without giving in to hatred or resentment, that you can support the hope of all citizens and encourage the irrepressible need for order and civil peace."

Christians in law enforcement, in particular, are to serve with genuine concern for the common good, he told members of the Catholic Police Guild of England and Wales in 1985. "I hope that your work, which sometimes brings you into contact with the darker side of human nature, will not deter you from enthusiastically serving the cause of civic harmony and well-being with sensitivity and Christian hope."

The Los Angeles Police Department, which provided massive security for John Paul's 1987 visit to that city, recorded a substantial drop in crime during the forty-seven hours the pope was in the city. Police Chief Daryl Gates noted that "there was a sense of calm that came to the City. People had time to reflect on what life is all about."

33 **Honoring Firefighters.** Tears flowed when John Paul accepted the helmet of New York City Fire Department chaplain Father Mychal Judge, just two months after the priest died during the 9/11 terrorist attacks in 2001. Speaking in English, the pope told the group from New York: "I offer a warm welcome to the delegation from the New York City Fire Department, so many of whose members lost their lives in the terrorist attack of September 11. May Almighty God grant the bereaved families consolation and peace, and may he give you and your fellow firefighters strength and courage to carry on your great service to your City."

This wasn't the first time John Paul addressed firefighters. He did so numerous times, including in a lengthy 1985 address in Italian to an international group of volunteer firefighters. He told them, "In a society riddled with numerous phenomena of selfishness and cruelty to the detriment of man, volunteering … is one of the positive signs of our time." Likening their work to that of the Good Samaritan, he asserted that the "willingness to sacrifice that [the first responders'] 'mission' requires, not infrequently in situations of grave personal danger and sometimes risk for the same will never be praised enough." In a 1989 address to Parisian firefighters, he again likened the work of firefighters to that of the Good Samaritan, saying, "You know that this man who goes to the aid of a victim left by the roadside is not only an example for us, he is also the very figure of Christ, the Savior of men!"

In 1997, John Paul honored Italian firefighter Mario Trematore, who broke through four layers of bulletproof glass to save the Shroud of Turin from a fire that roared through Turin's San Giovanni Cathedral, which houses the most famous relic of Christ's Passion.

32 **Concern for Military Personnel.** There is a good reason John Paul was mentioned numerous times as a frontrunner for the Nobel Peace Prize: he strongly opposed armed conflict throughout his pontificate. His consistent mantra was "No to war!" He was unrelenting in his opposition to the 1991 Persian Gulf War, calling it a "darkness [that had] cast a shadow over the whole human community."

However, his tone when he addressed troops was significantly different. John Paul's father was a military man, so the pope understood that soldiers do not create war but rather work to end conflict by securing peace. The military must "not take the form of a war apparatus of aggression, but rather as a force at the exclusive service of defending the security and freedom of peoples," he said to participants in an international meeting of military orders in 1994. "To evangelize the world of the Armed Forces means, in this sense, to make the military aware of the new way of conceiving its role, so that the soldier appears to public opinion even as a peace operator."

The pope also showed great concern for the spiritual care of those in military service. In 1986, he elevated the status of military "vicariates" to "ordinariates," essentially creating military dioceses. His apostolic constitution *Spirituali Militum Curae* recognized that military people "have need of a concrete and specific form of pastoral assistance." In a 1992 address to military chaplains, John Paul encouraged them to embrace their role as peacemaker in the midst of conflict: "Dear Chaplains, both in war and in peace may you be *always and only pastors of souls.* Be close to those entrusted to you. Help them with your prayer and exhort them to carry out with generosity the task assigned to them … that others will enjoy security and peace."

31 **Standing Up to the Mafia.** In 2019, a former New York Mafioso claimed that the death of Pope John Paul I in 1978 was a murder and that he had assisted in it because the new pope was about to expose the mob's stock fraud. The gangster also alleged that John Paul II had been spared because the Polish pope agreed not to reveal their crimes connected to the Vatican Bank. The story doesn't ring true. John Paul II was fearless in denouncing organized crime — even in the killers' own backyard.

On numerous visits to Sicily and other mob-controlled regions of southern Italy, the pope laid into those who exploit and murder for profit. In May 1993, after celebrating Mass in Agrigento, Sicily, John Paul made unscripted remarks demanding that the Mafiosi change their ways and convert or face God's wrath in the final Judgment. After that speech, bombs exploded in two Rome churches — including the pope's cathedral, Saint John Lateran — and the mob gunned down a priest in his own church. Just over a year later, the pope returned to Sicily and again took aim at the killers. "Those who are responsible for violence and arrogance stained by human blood will have to answer before the justice of God," he said. "Today, there is a strong yearning in Sicily to be redeemed and liberated, especially from the power of the Mafia."

John Paul's fearlessness surprised no one. He had stood up to violent Soviet communists in his native Poland (#30), and he had also condemned mob violence in Northern Ireland during "the Troubles," a conflict that spawned violence from the 1960s through the '90s. "Peace cannot be established by violence; peace can never flourish in a climate of terror, intimidation and death," he said.

30 **1979 Visit to Poland.** Wojtyła had only been in the Chair of Peter for eight months, but the fall of communism began the moment he set foot on Polish soil for the first time as pope, knelt down, and kissed the ground. John Paul II's initial visit to his homeland was the mighty first blow to crack the Iron Curtain and send it crumbling into the dustbin of history. That story is told more fully in The Fall of Communism (#4). As a prelude, let's explore what have been called "Nine Days That Changed the World."

After his election on October 16, 1978, John Paul had an immediate desire to return to his homeland. Cardinal Stefan Wyszyński set the wheels in motion by extending an invitation to the pope and lobbying the government to allow the pope's "pilgrimage." His return the following June coincided with the nine hundredth anniversary of national hero Saint Stanislaus's martyrdom. The nine-day visit to six cities also coincided with Pentecost — the feast celebrating the birthday of the Church and the descent of the Holy Spirit upon the apostles and Blessed Mother.

When John Paul II touched down in Warsaw on June 2, the vigil of Pentecost, the city was abuzz. Hundreds of thousands jammed the route from the airport to the inner city, and three million in total turned out to see him that day. Thirteen million saw him in person over his nine-day pilgrimage, and tens of millions more watched on television, despite the fact that broadcasters, all controlled by the government, refused to show young people, families, and large crowds.

"Christ cannot be kept out of the history of man in any part of the globe," the pope said to thunderous applause in his homily on that first day. "The exclusion of Christ from the history of man is an act against man. Without Christ it is impossible to understand the history of Poland." Many understood his words as a direct challenge to communist rule. He ended the homily by calling down the Holy Spirit upon his native land, which had suffered five years of Nazi occupation followed by thirty-three years of communist rule: "And I cry — I who am a Son of the land of Poland and who am also Pope John Paul II — I cry from all the depths of this Millennium, I cry on the vigil of Pentecost: Let your Spirit descend. Let your Spirit descend and renew the face of the earth, the face of *this land!*" Throughout the pope's homily, the crowd rhythmically chanted, "We want God! We want God!"

To Poles held captive for two generations, John Paul preached freedom of political self-determination, but he primarily preached the liberty to embrace Jesus Christ. The government's best efforts to control the message, minimize the papal visit, and break the Polish people's passion for their faith failed miserably.

29 **Empowering the Laity.** One of the Second Vatican Council's primary objectives was to empower the laity, and John Paul II took that assignment to heart (#9). In his 1988 post-synodal apostolic exhortation *Christifideles Laici* (On the Vocation and the Mission of the Lay Faithful in the Church and in the World), he wrote, "Through their participation in the *prophetic mission* of Christ, 'who proclaimed the kingdom of his Father by the testimony of his life ... ' the lay faithful are given the ability and responsibility to accept the gospel in faith and to proclaim it in word and deed, without hesitating to courageously identify and denounce evil."

For most of the Church's history, the laity were essentially content to allow the clergy and hierarchy to run Church affairs. Vatican II intended to change that by helping the laity understand that Jesus' command to proclaim the Good News is not meant just for those in holy orders. The laity, John Paul taught, are coresponsible for the Church: "Because of the one dignity flowing from Baptism, each member of the lay faithful, together with ordained ministers and men and women religious, shares a responsibility for the Church's mission."

Not only did the pope encourage lay individuals, he also spurred lay movements to take up the cause of evangelization (#1). "[Ecclesial movements] represent one of the most significant fruits of that springtime in the Church which was foretold by the Second Vatican Council," he told the first World Congress of Ecclesial Movements and New Communities in 1998. "Their presence is encouraging because it shows that this springtime is advancing and revealing the freshness of the Christian experience based on personal encounter with Christ."

28 **Faustina Kowalska.** After young Karol Wojtyła finished high school in his hometown of Wadowice, he and his father moved to Kraków in August 1938 so the teenager could start his studies at the Jagiellonian University. A few months later, thirty-three-year-old Faustina Kowalska died in Kraków. The young nun and the future pope never met, but their paths certainly crossed in mystical ways.

The Nazis closed the Jagiellonian when they took over Poland in 1939, arresting a large number of employees. The following year, Wojtyła worked at a stone quarry near the convent where Faustina had lived. Her Divine Mercy message (#2) had already begun to spread like wildfire throughout Poland. Later, as archbishop of Kraków, "Wojtyła ... defended Sister Faustina when her orthodoxy was being posthumously questioned in Rome, due in large part to a faulty Italian translation of her diary," writes George Weigel. In fact, Wojtyła tasked one of his top theologians with authenticating Faustina's diary. Six months to the day after the Holy See lifted the prohibition of her Divine Mercy message, Wojtyła was elected bishop of Rome.

John Paul proclaimed Faustina the first saint of the jubilee year, canonizing her on April 30, 2000, at a Mass this author attended. The pope said, "And you, Faustina, a gift of God to our time, a gift from the land of Poland to the whole Church, obtain for us an awareness of the depth of Divine Mercy; help us to have a living experience of it and to bear witness to it among our brothers and sisters." After the Mass, the Holy Father reportedly told his guests that this was the happiest day of his life. It certainly was the icing on the cake of John Paul's efforts to fulfill Jesus' demand to make his mercy known to the whole world.

27 **Maximilian Kolbe.** As with Faustina, John Paul II never met Maximilian Kolbe, the Polish Franciscan priest who volunteered to die in place of another man at a Nazi death camp in 1941. Wojtyła was inspired by Kolbe's love for Our Lady, his zeal for evangelization, and his courage in the face of tyranny. Cardinal Dziwisz writes that Faustina and Kolbe were actually "almost as dear to him as family members."

Kolbe was a legend in Poland and Japan long before his martyrdom. In both countries, he had founded a monastery and a town as well as Catholic radio stations and printing operations. All were dedicated to Jesus' mother, Mary. When Paul VI beatified the martyr in 1971, Cardinal Wojtyła gave a news conference in Rome "in which he said that Kolbe's priestly self-sacrifice had consisted not only in offering his life for another, but in the fact that he helped the nine other men condemned with him to die with a measure of dignity. Father Kolbe's spirit of forgiveness, the cardinal concluded, 'broke the infernal cycle of hatred.'"

On his first trip to Poland as pope, John Paul visited Auschwitz and kissed the floor of the cell where Kolbe died. At a Mass he celebrated at Auschwitz, he said, "It is well known that I have been here many times. So many times! And many times I have gone down to Maximilian Kolbe's death cell and kneeled in front of the execution wall and passed among the ruins of the cremation furnaces of Birkenau. It was impossible for me not to come here as Pope."

John Paul surprised many in 1982 when he waived the necessity for a second miracle for Kolbe's canonization. He also declared him a martyr even though a panel of Vatican cardinals had voted to the contrary. "It was necessary to take into consideration many voices of the People of God — especially of our Brothers in the episcopate of both Poland and Germany — who asked that Maximilian Kolbe be proclaimed as a martyr saint."

26 **Development of Personalism.** John Paul II advanced personalism as an intellectual discipline emphasizing the importance of the human person. Personalism was of utmost importance in his philosophy and in his social teaching; the intrinsic value and dignity of each unique and unrepeatable human person ran like a golden thread through all his writings, both before and after his election as pope.

"The person is a good towards which the only proper and adequate attitude is love," he wrote in 1960. As a professor of ethics at the University of Lublin, he delivered a paper in 1961 on "Thomistic Personalism," in which he wrote that Thomas paid too little attention to the human person as experienced from within. Wojtyła's personalism was confirmed and deepened during his experience at the Second Vatican Council (#9). He played a significant role in writing *Gaudium et Spes* (Pastoral Constitution on the Church in the Modern World), which speaks of "the exalted dignity proper to the human person" and of universal, inviolable human rights. The document also states that humans are the only creatures that God wills for their own sake, noting that they cannot rise to their full stature except through a disinterested gift of self.

The brutality of the twentieth century, rife with war and genocide, John Paul argued, "was due to an unwillingness to recognize the inherent value of the human person, who is made in the image and likeness of God, who confers upon it inalienable rights that can neither be bestowed nor withdrawn by any human power." The Holy Father wrote that "man receives from God his essential dignity and with it the capacity to transcend every social order so as to move towards truth and goodness."

25 **Resistance to Capital Punishment.** Throughout her history, the Church had upheld the use of the death penalty to defend society from evildoers, as a deterrent against crime, and as just retribution for grave evil. When the *Catechism of the Catholic Church* (#5) was first published in 1992, it discouraged authorities from capital punishment. However, five years later, John Paul ordered an update of paragraph 2267 limiting the use of the death penalty to circumstances where it was the "only possible way of effectively defending human lives against the unjust aggressor."

That revision was drawn from his 1994 encyclical *Evangelium Vitae* (On the Value and Inviolability of Human Life), in which he wrote that "as a result of steady improvements in the organization of the penal system, such cases are very rare, if not practically non-existent." According George Weigel, John Paul had a "loathing" for "the state's power of execution," and *Evangelium Vitae*'s "silence about the traditional arguments from retributive justice and deterrence seemed likely to fuel further debate on the issue."

In 1999, John Paul told a gathering in St. Louis that "a sign of hope is the increasing recognition that the dignity of human life must never be taken away. ... Modern society has the means of protecting itself, without definitively denying criminals the chance to reform. I renew the appeal I made most recently at Christmas for a consensus to end the death penalty, which is both cruel and unnecessary."

During the Jubilee Year 2000, the pope lobbied around the world for an end to capital punishment. At Rome's Regina Coeli Prison, he prayed: "May the death penalty, an unworthy punishment still used in some countries, be abolished throughout the world." In 2018, Pope Francis decreed that the death penalty is "inadmissible." Paragraph 2267 of the *Catechism* has been updated once again to reflect this language.

24 **Friendship with Joseph Ratzinger.** Not only was Cardinal Joseph Ratzinger John Paul II's longtime collaborator and immediate successor, but the men were also close friends. The future popes — the philosopher (Wojtyła) and the theologian (Ratzinger) — met for the first time at the 1978 conclave that elected Pope John Paul I. "I was particularly impressed by his human warmth and the deep inner rooting in God which appeared so clearly," the future Pope Benedict XVI said of that meeting. "And then, of course, I was also impressed by his philosophical education, his acuteness as a thinker and his ability to communicate his knowledge."

Shortly after becoming pope, John Paul asked Ratzinger to work with him in Rome. But the newly minted German cardinal declined, having been archbishop of Munich for little more than eighteen months. The pope renewed his offer in 1982. This time Ratzinger accepted, taking a number of roles at the Vatican, including prefect of the Congregation for the Doctrine of the Faith, a post he held until being elected John Paul's successor in 2005.

The two men's partnership over the course of the next twenty-three years was perhaps one of the greatest in modern Church history. "The collaboration with the Holy Father was always characterized by friendship and affection," Benedict XVI told an interviewer in 2013. "It developed above all on two planes: the official and the private." The two met every Friday at six o'clock in the evening to discuss work, but a deep friendship also developed. "[The idea] that John Paul II was a saint came to me from time to time, in the years of my collaboration with him, ever more clearly," Benedict said.

23 **Theological Legacy.** Few scholars disagree that John Paul II's academic strength was as a philosopher, whereas Ratzinger is a theologian. That said, John Paul had flexed his theological muscles long before collaborating with Ratzinger. In 1954, as a young priest, Wojtyła earned a doctorate in sacred theology from the Jagiellonian University and went on to teach moral philosophy and social ethics there. His papal theological works have made a tremendous impact on Church teaching.

Certainly, John Paul's seminal theological work is his Theology of the Body (#3), taught during his Wednesday audiences early in his pontificate. According to George Weigel, his 1993 encyclical *Veritatis Splendor* (The Splendor of Truth) "was intended to set a framework for the future development of an authentically Catholic moral theology. But *Veritatis Splendor* was not simply, or even primarily, John Paul's forceful entry into the intramural wars of Catholic moral theologians. Rather, it is best read as a crucial moment in the pope's quest for a new humanism, a reminder to men and women of the grandeur of the truth to which they can conform their lives and fulfill their destinies."

John Paul's legacy as an influential theologian, wrote Cardinal Avery Dulles, will be unpacked for centuries to come. Permeating the pope's theological works, Dulles found, is a profound understanding that our human dignity comes from our creation in the image and likeness of God. Dulles wrote that the Holy Father "brought the teaching of the church to bear on almost every area of modern life. While firmly adhering to the Catholic doctrinal tradition and the positions of Vatican II, he advanced Catholic teaching in several areas, such as the Theology of the Body, the sacredness of human life, the theological meaning of culture, work, and leisure."

22 **Expansion of the College of Cardinals.** With a papacy spanning several generations, it's no surprise that a large part of John Paul II's legacy is in the amazing number of bishops he appointed — and the 231 cardinals he created in nine consistories. He also called six full meetings of the College of Cardinals, the group tasked with advising him and electing his successor. He just missed out on elevating Joseph Ratzinger, who had been named a cardinal in 1977, but did place a red hat upon the head of Jorge Mario Bergoglio, who became Pope Francis in 2013.

John Paul fundamentally transformed the composition of the College of Cardinals to reflect the global nature of the Church. He shifted membership from Europe to the non-Western world, a practice continued by Benedict XVI and Francis. Outside the Roman Curia, "only 30 percent of John Paul II's cardinals hats were given to European bishops ... [so that] in 2005, the percentage of Italians in the college, which had been fairly consistent during the first half of the twentieth century, constituting around 50 percent of the college, fell to 17 percent by 2005."

John Paul's reorganization of the college, observed George Weigel, ensured that the election of his successor would be "one of the most open and complex of modern papal elections: the most open, because John Paul's recasting of the papacy in a far more evangelical and pastoral style helped make nationality a less important issue, perhaps even a nonissue; the most complex, because the men who will face the Herculean task of electing a successor ... don't know each other that well, come from a wide disparity of backgrounds and experiences, [and] don't have a single common language."

21 **The Church in China.** Most Catholics in the Western world are curiously unaware of John Paul II's extensive efforts to increase the Church's influence in China. "Concern for the Church in China," wrote the pope in 1982, "has become the particular and constant anxiety of my pontificate." During the 1990s, particularly during his trips to North Korea and the Philippines, he broadcast live radio messages to China, and he was in regular communication with Beijing.

China broke off diplomatic relations with the Holy See in 1951, but that didn't stop John Paul from making diplomatic and pastoral efforts. Appointment of Chinese bishops was one of the long-standing points of contention between the Chinese government and the Church. For decades, the communist-run Chinese Patriotic Catholic Association appointed its own bishops in the country without consulting the Holy Father.

"It is no secret that the Holy See, in the name of the whole Catholic Church and, I believe, for the benefit of the whole human family, hopes for the opening of some form of dialogue with the Authorities of the People's Republic of China," John Paul said in a 2001 speech. "Once the misunderstandings of the past have been overcome, such a dialogue would make it possible for us to work together for the good of the Chinese people and for peace in the world."

In his speeches and writing, John Paul referred to China at least sixty times. He addressed the Chinese people at least thirty times. Although he showed great concern for diplomatic relations with Beijing, his greater concern was for the spiritual well-being of Chinese Catholics. He saidL "[The Church] has no political or economic goals; she has no worldly mission. She wants to be, in China as in any other country, the herald of the Kingdom of God."

20 **The Dignity of Marriage.** As a young priest, Father Wojtyła spent some of his most formative moments with his *Rodzinka*, or "Little Family." It was here that he experienced young men and women falling in love, getting married, and having children. Before long, he had turned those experiences into a marriage formation program, followed by a groundbreaking book.

"In 1950, he launched at Saint Florian's the first marriage-preparation program in the history of the Archdiocese of Kraków," writes George Weigel. "Wojtyła set out to create a pastoral program that systematically prepared young couples for Christian marriage and family life through religious reflection, theological education, and a frank exploration of the practical and personal difficulties and opportunities of married life and child rearing." *Time* magazine called the program "perhaps the most successful marriage institute in Christianity, set up to deal with the problems of marital discord, family planning, illegitimacy and venereal disease, alcoholism, wife beating and child abuse."

This was the era of American "sexologist" Dr. Alfred Kinsey, who conducted highly flawed experiments that laid the groundwork for the "culture of death," which Wojtyła would battle as bishop and pope (#8). While Kinsey rejected time-tested sexual ethics and mores like lifelong marriage, monogamy, and chastity, Wojtyła verified that these are the very foundations of civil society. His work included thousands of hours in the confessional and in spiritual direction. The fruit of that work was *Love and Responsibility*, published in 1960. George Weigel writes that the book "cast a new light on classic Christian sexual ethics, giving the Church's teaching on sexuality, marriage, and responsible family planning a new, rich, humanistic texture."

The Holy Father's magnum opus on marriage and family — his 1981 apostolic exhortation *Familiaris Consortio* (On the Role of the Christian Family in the Modern World) — addresses modernity's challenge to God's plan for marriage and proposes solutions to overcoming a hostile culture. It will help guide Catholic thought on the subject for centuries.

This author came to better understand John Paul's commitment to fostering holy marriages on trips to Rome in the late 1990s, during which I always made it a point to attend his Wednesday general audience, held either in the Paul VI Hall or in Saint Peter's Square. These short gatherings included a talk from the pope and his greetings to visiting groups. Next, he would bless the sick and then a queue of brides and grooms in their wedding clothes. I resolved to take part in that parade one day. The final time I kissed his ring was with my wife at my side in 2002, just eleven days after our wedding.

19 **Defense of the Family.** When he canonized John Paul II in 2014, Pope Francis called him the "pope of the family" — and for good reason. Family and community, John Paul wrote, are inextricably linked: "The parents create the family as a complement to and extension of their love. To create a family means to create a community."

Family is the "domestic church," John Paul taught. He challenged parents to build a faith-filled environment where their children would learn their true identity as adopted sons and daughters of God. In a 1995 homily, he said, "Catholic parents must learn to form their family as a 'domestic Church,' *a church in the home* as it were, where God is honored, his law is respected, prayer is a normal event, virtue is transmitted by word and example, and everyone shares the hopes, the problems and sufferings of everyone else. All this is not to advocate a return to some outdated style of living: it is to return to *the roots of human development and human happiness!*"

More than ever, he said, families need to be grounded in prayer. In *Familiaris Consortio*, he wrote, "At a moment of history in which the family is the object of numerous forces that seek to destroy it ... the Church perceives in a more urgent and compelling way her mission of proclaiming to all people the plan of God for marriage and the family, ensuring their full vitality and human and Christian development, and thus contributing to the renewal of society." John Paul understood the big picture and wrote with urgency: "*The future of humanity passes by way of the family.* It is therefore indispensable and urgent that every person of good will should endeavor to save and foster the values and requirements of the family."

18 The Gift of Motherhood. John Paul was not quite nine years old when his mother, Emilia Kaczorowska Wojtyła, died of kidney disease and congestive heart failure. Some have suggested that the future pope's Marian piety grew out of the loss of his mother, though there's little real evidence of that. However, there is significant evidence that he saw motherhood as a great gift to be revered, one that he usually explained in relationship to the Blessed Mother, in whom the Church finds the highest expression of the feminine genius.

"Each and every time that *motherhood* is repeated in human history, it is always *related to the Covenant* which God established with the human race through the motherhood of the Mother of God," he wrote in *Mulieris Dignitatem* (On the Dignity and Vocation of Women) in 1981. The pope also taught that each father owes "*a special debt to the woman*" who bears his child. He wrote, "Motherhood involves a special communion with the mystery of life, as it develops in the woman's womb. The mother is filled with wonder at this mystery of life, and 'understands' with unique intuition what is happening inside her."

John Paul heaped praise on women who sacrifice much to become mothers — including women who do not bear children but are nonetheless called to "spiritual motherhood": "*[T]he Church gives thanks for each and every woman: for mothers, for sisters, for wives; for women consecrated to God in virginity; for women dedicated to the many human beings who await the gratuitous love of another person; for women who watch over the human persons in the family, which is the fundamental sign of the human community; for women who work professionally, and who at times are burdened by a great social responsibility; for 'perfect' women and for 'weak' women — for all women as they have come forth from the heart of God in all the beauty and richness of their femininity.*"

17 **Protection for the Unborn.** John Paul II was among the strongest voices for the pro-life movement. He left us an extraordinary, lifelong teaching on the inalienable dignity of the human person. He coined the phrases "culture of life" (#8) and "culture of death" and raised the subject with politicians who support the slaughter of innocents through abortion.

In 1994, "the Pope almost singlehandedly derailed the plans of the Clinton administration and the U.S. government to have abortion on demand declared a universal human right, akin to religious liberty" at the United Nations' conference on population and development, to which the Holy See sent a sizable delegation. "Abortion, which destroys existing human life, is a heinous evil, and it is never an acceptable method of family planning," John Paul said in his letter to the secretary general of the conference. The Holy See's delegation to the Beijing conference in 1995 also vigorously defended the unborn.

John Paul's commitment to the cause of life was unwavering from the beginning, and it became a hallmark of his pontificate. "It is not a question of imposing Christian principles on everyone, as some people have objected, but of defending a fundamental human right, that is, the right to life," he told Poland's bishops in 1993. His preeminent defense of human life came in his 1995 encyclical *Evangelium Vitae*. In it, he drew a connection (which should be obvious) between the commandment "Thou shalt not kill" and the unborn child. "When a parliamentary or social majority decrees that it is legal, at least under certain conditions, to kill unborn human life," he wrote, "is it not really making a 'tyrannical' decision with regard to the weakest and most defenceless of human beings?"

16 **Care for the Elderly.** John Paul II truly was a "whole-life" leader. He taught the inviolable worth and dignity of each human person from conception to natural death, and he did so forcefully and unapologetically, particularly in *Evangelium Vitae*. He wrote, "The taking of life not yet born or in its final stages is sometimes marked by a mistaken sense of altruism and human compassion[.] ... [S]uch a culture of death ... ends up by becoming the freedom of 'the strong' against the weak who have no choice but to submit."

As he grew older, the pope addressed the aged specifically. At seventy-nine, he wrote in a letter to the elderly, "I wish simply to express my spiritual closeness to you as someone who, with the passing of years, has come to a deeper personal understanding of this phase of life." The pope went on to condemn euthanasia as "an intrinsically evil act" but noted that it is morally permissible for the terminally ill to reject "aggressive medical treatment." He continued, "When God permits us to suffer because of illness, loneliness or other reasons associated with old age, he always gives us the grace and strength to unite ourselves with greater love to the sacrifice of his Son and to share ever more fully in his plan of salvation."

Three years later, the pope sent a letter to the Second World Assembly on Aging in Madrid. "The elderly should never be considered a burden on society, but a resource which can contribute to society's well-being," he said. "It is not just a question of doing something for older people but also of accepting them in a realistic way as partners in shared projects — at the level of thought, dialogue and action. ... The elderly constitute an important school of life, capable of transmitting values and traditions, and of fostering the growth of younger generations, who thus learn to seek not only their own good but also that of others."

15 **"Saint Maker."** Critics accused John Paul II of turning the Vatican into a "saint factory." He responded by reminding us of the universal call to holiness — that all are called to be saints. He also clarified on numerous occasions that the Church does not "make" saints; she merely recognizes saints that God has made.

Over the course of his papacy, John Paul canonized 482 saints — more than all popes of the previous 500 years combined — and beatified 1,341 men and women. From his perspective, the more the merrier! He canonized some of the most memorable saints in modern history, including Padre Pio, Faustina Kowalska, Maximilian Kolbe, Edith Stein, Katharine Drexel, and Gianna Beretta Molla.

It's important to remember that John Paul was raised in Poland, where a devotion to the saints is as natural as breathing, so part of his mission as bishop and pope was to promote this devotion. At a 1977 synod on religious education, Wojtyła noted that "'the saints were the best catechists' because effective religious education took place not simply through the transmission of ideas, but through the example of heroic virtue."

The understanding that all are called to be saints, John Paul taught, is an essential part of the New Evangelization (#1). *"The universal call to holiness* is closely linked to the *universal call to mission.* Every member of the faithful is called to holiness and to mission," he wrote in 1990. That call became part of his mantra: "Do not be afraid to be saints! This is the liberty with which Christ has set us free," he said at the 1989 World Youth Day. *"Dear young people, let yourselves be won by him!"*

14 *The Splendor of Truth.* Not only did John Paul II write an encyclical on truth (*Veritatis Splendor*), but he made truth a major theme of his priesthood and pontificate. In fact, during an "intervention" at the Second Vatican Council, he famously said, *"Non datur libertas sine veritate"* ("There is no liberty without truth"). George Weigel writes that "for Karol Wojtyła, who had long been convinced that truth is liberating, the 'limitations' of the papacy were not constraints at all. The truth that binds and frees at the same time was, in his judgment, an instrument for exercising the Office of Peter in service to human freedom."

John Paul taught that truth and freedom are forever connected because they are both found in the person of Jesus Christ. People, he wrote, are created with an innate desire to know the Lord. He opened his 1998 encyclical *Fides et Ratio* with these words: "Faith and reason are like two wings on which the human spirit rises to the contemplation of truth; and God has placed in the human heart a desire to know the truth — in a word, to know himself — so that, by knowing and loving God, men and women may also come to the fullness of truth about themselves." He continued, "Once the truth is denied to human beings, it is pure illusion to try to set them free. Truth and freedom either go together hand in hand or together they perish in misery."

Sin darkens our ability to recognize truth, he said, but a heart open to God is open to truth. Christ "has called you and chosen you to live in the freedom of the children of God," he told young people at World Youth Day in 1997. "Turn to Him in prayer and in love. Ask him to grant you the courage and strength to live in this freedom always. Walk with Him who is 'the Way, the Truth and the Life'!"

13 **Revised Code of Canon Law.** After Pope John XXIII was elected in 1958, one of his major initiatives was to revise the Church's complex legal system. That revision took a back seat to the Second Vatican Council, which began in 1962. Revisions to the Code of Canon Law moved slowly until John Paul II kickstarted the process in 1982.

That year, he met with seven canonical experts from different countries. "At a working lunch, John Paul told the group that he had read the entire draft Code twice, and wanted them to meet with him to go over the entire project, canon by canon, so that he understood exactly what was being said in each of the 1,752 laws and their various subsections." Things moved quickly, and the revised Code was promulgated eleven months later. The first of three major legislative initiatives in John Paul II's pontificate, it was followed by the 1988 apostolic constitution *Pastor Bonus* (The Good Shepherd), which reformed the Roman Curia, and the revised Code of Oriental Canon Law in 1990 for the Eastern Catholic Churches.

John Paul said that the 1983 revised Code was Vatican II's final document. The new Code is the second comprehensive codification of the Latin Church's nonliturgical laws, replacing the Code promulgated in 1917. The pope wrote, "The Code of Canon Law is extremely necessary for the Church. Since, indeed, it is organized as a social and visible structure, it must also have norms: in order that its hierarchical and organic structure be visible; in order that the exercise of the functions divinely entrusted to her, especially that of sacred power and of the administration of the sacraments, may be adequately organized."

12 **World Travel.** When, in 1964, Paul VI became the first pope ever to fly in an airplane, he broke the mold. Prior to that, no pope had ever left Europe, and none had left Italy since 1809. If Paul VI broke the mold, John Paul II shattered it. He racked up more miles aboard "Shepherd One" than all of his predecessors combined — and likely his successors for years to come.

All told, the Polish pontiff made 104 foreign trips, touching down in 129 countries (two-thirds of all nations on the planet). He logged more than 775,000 miles — the equivalent of circling the globe more than thirty times. George Weigel reports, "In addition, John Paul made 146 visits within Italy itself, not counting 748 visits within the Diocese of Rome or to Castel Gandolfo, in the course of which he met with all but sixteen of Rome's 336 parishes."

Most historians agree that John Paul was seen in person by more people than anyone in history. One observed that "difficult political situations were no deterrent to papal travel: for example, John Paul II was the only major head of state to visit East Timor during its brutal occupation by Indonesia (consequently, many East Timorese men born after the visit are named John Paul)."

The concept of papal press conferences in the air began with John Paul's first trip abroad. The pope, who referred to his travels as "pilgrimages," brought along both the Gospel and a sense of humor. A reporter once asked him if he ever got tired during his trips. "No," he replied, "I'm trying to make everyone else tired." When asked if he traveled too much, John Paul quipped, "Yes ... but sometimes it is necessary to do something of what is too much!"

11 **Devotion to the Eucharist.** John Paul II drew strength from Jesus' true presence in the Blessed Sacrament, the source and summit of the Faith. He regularly lay prostrate before the tabernacle with his arms stretched out to the side so that his body formed a cross. He groaned as he prayed, often in a mystical, trancelike state. The Holy Sacrifice of the Mass, he taught, unites heaven and earth. At the beginning of the 2004–2005 Year of the Eucharist, he said, "The Eucharist is a great mystery! And it is one which above all must be *well celebrated*. Holy Mass needs to be set at the centre of the Christian life and celebrated in a dignified manner by every community."

He consistently urged the faithful, particularly priests, to learn to know Jesus better by spending time with him in the Blessed Sacrament, particularly after Mass. "From this moment on, live the Eucharist fully; be persons for whom the Holy Mass, Communion, and Eucharistic adoration are the center and summit of their whole life. Offer Christ your heart in meditation and personal prayer which is the foundation of the spiritual life," he told Spanish seminarians in 1982.

Prior to his papacy, he attended two International Eucharistic Congresses. As pope, he convened seven, attending most of them in person. He wrote a letter on the Eucharist to the world's bishops in 1980, and his final encyclical, *Ecclesia de Eucharistia* (On the Eucharist and Its Relationship to the Church), focused on the Blessed Sacrament. "Every commitment to holiness, every activity aimed at carrying out the Church's mission, every work of pastoral planning, must draw the strength it needs from the Eucharistic mystery," he wrote.

10 **Devotion to Mary.** John Paul II had an intense devotion to the Blessed Mother. His school teacher noted that sixteen-year-old Wojtyła would write "To Jesus through Mary" or "Jesus, Mary, and Joseph" at the top of every page he submitted. His papal motto — *Totus Tuus* ("Completely Yours") — expressed his devotion to Jesus' mother; it was based on Saint Louis-Marie Grignion de Montfort's prayer of dedication to Mary. John Paul's papal motto and papal coat of arms, which features a capital *M* for "Mary," both date back to his time as auxiliary bishop of Kraków.

De Montfort, a French priest of the late seventeenth and early eighteenth centuries, was key to Wojtyła's early formation and to his Marian devotion. During Nazi Germany's occupation of Poland, the future pope worked for a time as a laborer at the Solvay chemical plant in Kraków while secretly studying for the priesthood. He "read and reread many times" the writings of de Montfort. "I then realized that I could not exclude the Mother of the Lord from my life without disregarding the will of God-the-Trinity, who wanted to 'begin and complete' the great mysteries of salvation history with the responsible and faithful collaboration of the humble Handmaid of Nazareth," he told the Eighth International Mariological Colloquium in 2000.

In high school, Wojtyła joined the Sodality of Mary, a society of young men dedicated to fostering Marian devotion; he served two terms as the group's president. He later questioned if this devotion detracted from his focus on Jesus, but de Montfort's writing, particularly *True Devotion to Mary*, convinced him that she always leads people to her son.

As a delegate to the Second Vatican Council, Bishop Wojtyła, together with the Polish hierarchy, tried to convince bishops to include a "separate conciliar document on the Blessed Virgin Mary, a position the council would eventually reject for theological and ecumenical reasons." However, the council incorporated its statement on Mary into *Lumen Gentium* (Dogmatic Constitution on the Church).

John Paul's papal teaching on Our Lady contains dozens of speeches and documents, including the encyclical *Redemptoris Mater* (On the Blessed Virgin Mary in the Life of the Pilgrim Church; 1987), a Marian Year (1987–1988), and a letter on the Rosary (#6). He acknowledged Our Lady's unique role in salvation history and her unique intercessory ability. "If the mystery of the Word made flesh enables us to glimpse the mystery of the divine motherhood and ... contemplation of the Mother of God brings us to a more profound understanding of the mystery of the Incarnation, then the same must be said for the mystery of the Church and Mary's role in the work of salvation," he wrote in *Redemptoris Mater*. And he proposed to the world a new set of mysteries for the Holy Rosary in his 2002 apostolic letter *Rosarium Virginis Mariae* (#6).

The Blessed Mother "has been given to us as a model in our pilgrimage of faith," he said during his first visit to the United States. "From Mary we learn to surrender to God's will in all things. From Mary, we learn to trust even when all hope seems gone. From Mary, we learn to love Christ, her Son and the Son of God. For Mary is not only the Mother of God, she is Mother of the Church as well." The pope also believed that Mary played a role in saving his life during the 1981 assassination attempt (#84): "One hand pulled the trigger, and another guided the bullet." That bullet is now welded into the crown of the statue of Mary in Fátima.

9 **Unpacking Vatican II.** As a young bishop, Wojtyła was summoned to Rome for the opening sessions of the Second Vatican Council in 1962. He was one of four men in attendance who would later become bishop of Rome. He was also one of the youngest bishops in the world at forty-two years old. The junior bishop sat about five hundred feet from the high altar of Saint Peter's Basilica, but by the time the council concluded in 1965, George Weigel recounts, "Wojtyła had become a significant figure in the council's deliberations, playing important roles in developing Vatican II's text on religious freedom and the vocation of the laity; he also helped draft one of the council's most controversial documents, the Pastoral Constitution on the Church in the Modern World."

It wasn't until 1978 that Wojtyła met Cardinal Joseph Ratzinger, who had also served as an intellectual father of the council. Weigel writes that the two men "found themselves in what Ratzinger later recalled as a 'spontaneous sympathy' for each other's sense of what was needed to secure the legacy of Vatican II."

When he was elected pope, only thirteen years after the council's closing, John Paul II inherited a deeply divided Church. One faction proclaimed the "Spirit of Vatican II," while another thought the council was a terrible mistake. The pope understood immediately that his task would be to interpret and unpack the council. In 2001, he wrote, "From the beginning of my Pontificate, my thoughts had been on this Holy Year 2000 as an important appointment. I thought of its celebration as a providential opportunity during which the Church, thirty-five years after the Second Vatican Ecumenical Council, would examine how far she had renewed herself, in order to be able to take up her evangelizing mission with fresh enthusiasm."

John Paul confronted critics who contended that the council was a rupture from historic Church teaching — a "hermeneutic of discontinuity." The genuine intent of the council fathers must never be disregarded by the Church, he told a conference studying Vatican II's implementation in 2000: "To interpret the council on the supposition that it marks a break with the past, when in reality *it stands in continuity with the faith of all times*, is a definite mistake. What has been believed by 'everyone, always and everywhere' is the authentic newness that enables every era to perceive the light that comes from the word of God's Revelation in Jesus Christ."

John Paul made reference to the council and its documents in the vast majority of his writing and speaking. He made it his mission to ensure that the proper interpretation and implementation of the council occurred on his watch. Biographer George Weigel emphatically asserts that John Paul's pontificate brought the council's teachings into the twenty-first century: "His pontificate made clear that Vatican II was to be understood as a council in continuity with the Church's tradition, not a rupture with that tradition. The Church was to engage the modern world with its own distinctive resources of mind, heart and spirit."

The Holy Father himself called Vatican II "*truly a prophetic message for the Church's life; it will continue to be so for many years in the third millennium.* ... The Church, rich in the eternal truths entrusted to her, will still speak to the world, proclaiming that Jesus Christ is the one true Saviour of the world: yesterday, today and for ever!"

8 **Culture of Life.** Even as a young man in Poland, Karol Wojtyła was a culture warrior. He saw firsthand the destruction wreaked upon his country by totalitarian ideologies during both the Nazi and communist occupations of Poland; he then worked to build a culture of life in his homeland as a seminarian, priest, and bishop. Even though the culture of death dominated for a time, life prevailed because of the faithful witness of the Polish people — including that of their pope — leading to the fall of communism in Eastern Europe (#4).

John Paul II used the phrase "culture of life" to emphasize the inviolable dignity and worth of each person from conception to natural death. He contrasted it with the "culture of death" — the blatant disregard for human life seen in abortion, euthanasia, embryonic stem cell research, capital punishment, and the like.

As Christianity waned in practice and influence, particularly in the West, the pope saw that human life was cheapened. His first notable reference to a "culture of life" was in his 1991 encyclical *Centesimus Annus*, in which he said that morals and ethics must first be nurtured in the family: "The family is indeed sacred: it is the place in which life — the gift of God — can be properly welcomed and protected against the many attacks to which it is exposed, and can develop in accordance with what constitutes authentic human growth. In the face of the so-called culture of death, the family is the heart of the culture of life."

He also discussed the clash between the cultures of life and death during his 1993 farewell address at World Youth Day in Denver: "In our own century, as at no other time in history, the 'culture of death' has assumed a social and institutional form of legality to justify the most horrible crimes against humanity: genocide, 'final solutions,' 'ethnic cleansings,' and the massive 'taking of lives of human beings even before they are born, or before they reach the natural point of death.'"

As the cultural divide deepened and the disregard for life became more socially acceptable, John Paul in 1995 penned *Evangelium Vitae*, a document many regard as the best defense of human life since Paul VI's *Humanae Vitae.* "Man is called to a fullness of life which far exceeds the dimensions of his earthly existence, because it consists in sharing the very life of God," he wrote, calling on humanity to embrace heavenly values. "In our present social context, marked by a dramatic struggle between the 'culture of life' and the 'culture of death,' there is need to develop a deep critical sense, capable of discerning true values and authentic needs," he wrote. "Only when people are open to the fullness of the truth about God, man and history will the words 'You shall not kill' shine forth once more as a good for man in himself and in his relations with others."

Evangelium Vitae is the Magna Carta of the pro-life movement. Christians around the world — including Presidents Donald J. Trump and George W. Bush — began using the phrase "culture of life" to rail against the careless disregard for human life. "The taking of life not yet born or in its final stages is sometimes marked by a mistaken sense of altruism and human compassion," John Paul wrote. "Such a culture of death ... ends up by becoming the freedom of 'the strong' against the weak who have no choice but to submit."

7 **World Youth Day.** Karol Wojtyła was a people magnet. He drew young and old long before his papacy began in 1978. Even when he was a young priest, people flocked to him, especially young people. The memories of these modest youth gathering stayed with John Paul II into his papacy. After he met in 1980 with young people in Paris and had the 1984 Holy Year meeting with youth in Rome, the idea of a larger, international gathering began to develop. He invited youth back to Rome in 1985 — and a quarter of a million took him up on it.

> It was then decided to mark Palm Sunday, 1986, as the first "official" World Youth Day, and to celebrate it in the different dioceses around the world. Beginning in 1987, and continuing biennially, World Youth Day was celebrated with the Pope at an international venue to which the youth of the world would be invited — Buenos Aires in 1987, Santiago de Compostela in 1989, Częstochowa in 1991, Denver in 1993, Manila in 1995, and Paris in 1997, where the Pope announced that the next World Youth Day would be in Rome in 2000. On the even-numbered "off" years, World Youth Day is celebrated in the dioceses.

John Paul drew the largest crowd in human history — between five and seven million people — for World Youth Day in Manila.

While it's impossible to measure the full impact of World Youth Day, it's also impossible to ignore its fruit. The secular media predicted World Youth Day in Denver (1993) would be a bust. They thought that no sane young person — Catholic or otherwise — would trek to Colorado to listen to a seventy-three-year-old Polish pope. They were wrong! Denver was a massive success, with John Paul receiving a rock-star welcome at Mile High Stadium, and nearly a million people camped out for the final Mass in Cherry Creek Park.

"Do not be afraid to go out on the streets and into public

places, like the first apostles who preached Christ and the Good News of salvation in the squares of cities, towns and villages. This is no time to be ashamed of the Gospel. It is the time to preach it from the rooftops!" John Paul challenged in his homily, and American youth responded by embracing the Faith in droves. Denver became a beehive of Catholic activity in World Youth Day's wake. New apostolates like the Augustine Institute and the Fellowship of Catholic University Students (FOCUS) sprang up in the city, rising to the pope's challenge by embracing the New Evangelization (#1).

The World Youth Days have also borne vocational fruit. It's reasonable to believe that millions of young people have met their spouses through these gatherings since 1986 — along with untold thousands hearing their call to religious life. And countless others who have attended World Youth Day gatherings have come away committed to enjoying a vibrant sacramental life with a genuine, fruitful relationship with Jes Christ.

"Few, if any, Catholic initiatives since the Second Vatican Council have given so many Catholics a sense of themselves as members of the *communio* of a genuinely universal Church as John Paul II's World Youth Days," writes biographer George Weigel. "That was certainly one impact of Denver, and particularly for the young American pilgrims. Young people by the thousands also experienced a deeper connection to the Church's sacramental life."

6 **Luminous Mysteries of the Rosary.** The Rosary was John Paul II's favorite devotion. The pope didn't just pray a daily Rosary: he prayed many daily Rosaries. Given Saint Louis de Montfort's powerful influence on Wojtyła's devotion to Our Lady, it's no wonder he became known as "The Pope of the Rosary." Following each of this author's brief private audiences with John Paul, he pressed a rosary into my hand.

After the terror attacks on September 11, 2001, John Paul appealed "to all individuals and families and communities to pray the Rosary for peace, even daily, so that the world will be preserved from the dreadful scourge of terrorism." Throughout his ministerial life, he encouraged the faithful to pray the Rosary, writing, "I look to all of you, brothers and sisters of every state of life, to you, Christian families, to you, the sick and elderly, and to you, young people: *confidently take up the Rosary once again.*"

John Paul II declared the Great Jubilee of the Year 2000 to mark the beginning of the third millennium of Christianity with the primary goal of advancing the New Evangelization (#1). With the jubilee year in the rearview mirror, the pope declared a Year of the Rosary from October 2002 to October 2003, at the same time issuing the apostolic letter *Rosarium Virginis Mariae*, in which he reiterated that the Rosary, though Marian in character, is a meditation on the Gospel of Jesus Christ: "With the Rosary, the Christian people *sits at the school of Mary* and is led to contemplate the beauty on the face of Christ. ... The Rosary helps us to be conformed ever more closely to Christ until we attain true holiness."

In this letter, John Paul gave the Church a new set of five mysteries of the Rosary: the Mysteries of Light. The original fifteen mysteries contemplate Jesus' early life, his Passion and death, and his resurrection and the aftermath. Missing was a reflection upon his earthly ministry. The mid-twentieth-century Maltese priest Saint George Preca, beatified in 2001 by John Paul II and canonized in 2007 by Benedict XVI, filled in the rest, first publishing them in 1973. John Paul brought those mysteries to the faithful. The Mysteries of Light, or Luminous Mysteries, are Jesus' baptism, the wedding at Cana, the proclamation of the Kingdom, the Transfiguration, and the Last Supper (the institution of the Eucharist).

It's important to note that, contrary to popular belief, John Paul did not *impose* five new mysteries upon the Church. He *suggested* them — and the people of God overwhelmingly said yes! He wrote, "To bring out fully the Christological depth of the Rosary it would be suitable to make an addition to the traditional pattern which, while left to the freedom of individuals and communities, could broaden it to include *the mysteries of Christ's public ministry between his Baptism and his Passion.* In the course of those mysteries we contemplate important aspects of the person of Christ as the definitive revelation of God."

Taking a cue from Father Patrick Peyton, John Paul taught that the family that prays together stays together: "The Rosary is also, and always has been, *a prayer of and for the family.* At one time this prayer was particularly dear to Christian families, and it certainly brought them closer together. It is important not to lose this precious inheritance. We need to return to the practice of family prayer and prayer for families, continuing to use the Rosary."

5 The *Catechism of the Catholic Church.* With the tumult that followed the Second Vatican Council, both Paul VI and John Paul II fixed their attention on the necessity of unpacking the council and dealing with the dissent and rampant confusion left in its wake. To this end, John Paul convened an Extraordinary Synod of Bishops in 1985 to mark the twentieth anniversary of Vatican II's conclusion. In the synod's final report, John Paul approved three suggestions given by the bishops: the creation of a universal catechism of Catholic faith and morals; a study of the theological nature of bishops' conferences; and the publication of a new Code of Canon Law for the Eastern Catholic Churches.

Following the Council of Trent (1545–1563), called in response to the Protestant Reformation, the Church published the *Roman Catechism* in 1566; council fathers found it necessary to publish this document because both priests and the lay faithful at the time were poorly catechized. The *Roman Catechism* held sway for four hundred years, inspiring many national catechisms, including the *Baltimore Catechism*, which was used for instruction in the United States from 1885 until the late 1960s.

John Paul tasked a group of twelve bishops with creating the new catechism. The group was led primarily by Cardinal Joseph Ratzinger, then prefect of the Congregation for the Doctrine of the Faith, and Father Christoph Schönborn, who later became archbishop of Vienna. The result was an up-to-date, comprehensive declaration of Catholic beliefs. Although the writing and publication of the new *Catechism of the Catholic Church* were not without their challenges, John Paul approved and promulgated the text in 1992. It was first published in French (1992), then in English (1994) and Latin (1997). Unlike previous iterations, this catechism was not in question-and-answer format. The Vatican updated the text on the death penalty in 1997 and again in 2018.

According to a 1995 review, "The catechism covers the entire range of the faith: it contains all the tenets of the Catholic faith contained in Scripture and Tradition and authoritatively expounded by the magisterium of the Church. It sets forth these tenets of the faith, along with the essentials of what follows from these tenets, in short and remarkably lucid successively numbered articles — 2865 of them in all. Included in these numbered paragraphs is a veritable treasure trove of quotations from the fathers, doctors, and saints of the Church."

Critics inside the Church said that a universal catechism was an outdated idea, that there was no need for such a resource. But John Paul shot back that the *Catechism* was "indispensable, in order that the richness of the teaching of the Church following the Second Vatican Council could be preserved in a new synthesis and be given a new direction. Without the Catechism of the universal Church, this would not have been accomplished."

The faithful responded to the critics by making the *Catechism* an international bestseller, with well over eight million copies in print in twenty languages worldwide. According to George Weigel, the successful publication of the *Catechism* "was a clear statement that Catholicism thought it possible to account for its beliefs and practices in a coherent, comprehensive, and accessible way." Ultimately, the *Catechism* is an indispensable resource for catechesis and evangelization. It tells the "what" and "why" of Church teaching, and it sets the Catholic Church apart from other world religions. After all, what other major faith has published such a comprehensive volume of its beliefs and the reasons behind them?

4 **The Fall of Communism.** John Paul was perhaps more aware of the devastation caused by the flawed ideologies of the twentieth century than any other world leader of his era. He lived through the German domination of Poland, followed by communist occupation, which ended only after he exerted great personal effort along with some legendary collaborators to bring an end to the Soviet Union and its grip on Eastern Europe.

"Not only did the people reject nazism as a system aimed at the destruction of Poland, and communism as an oppressive system imposed from the East, but in the process of resistance, they also pursued highly positive ideals," John Paul wrote in his 2005 book *Memory and Identity*. Those ideals were key to communism's collapse in Eastern Europe. The first significant crack in the Iron Curtain began with John Paul's 1979 nine-day visit to his native Poland. He arrived with tremendous hope for his nation, inspiring his countrymen to turn to God and to fight for their right to freedom.

That unprecedented visit had a tremendous impact on Ronald Reagan, who was "never the same" after the pope's Poland visit. Reagan, who had not yet been elected president of the United States, recorded several nationally syndicated radio broadcasts on the pope's impact in Poland. "It has been a long time since we've seen a leader of such courage and such uncompromising dedication to simple morality — to the belief that right does make might," Reagan said. The future US president had found a kindred spirit in John Paul, someone willing to speak out against evil.

So how did the pope and the president — with some help from British prime minister Margaret Thatcher — bring an end to the "Evil Empire"? They had the temperament, the timing, the positions of power, and some help — divine and otherwise. The Soviet empire was crumbling from within. Its economy was weak for many reasons, not the least of which was that the Soviets were trying to keep up with the United States in the arms race. Most importantly, however, Reagan and John Paul were utterly convinced that they were on the right side of history. "The years ahead are great ones for this country, for the cause of freedom and the spread of civilization," Reagan said in 1981. "The West won't contain communism; it will transcend communism. It won't bother to dismiss or denounce it, it will dismiss it as some bizarre chapter in human history whose last pages are even now being written."

John Paul and Reagan met several times, and the governments they led shared a tremendous amount of intelligence concerning Poland and the Soviet Union. Envoys shuttled back and forth between Rome and Washington. For both men, however, this was far more a spiritual battle than a political one. John Paul supported the Polish Solidarity movement, and he railed against atheistic communism in his first encyclical, *Redemptor Hominis*, published only five months into his pontificate. He wrote, "Certainly the curtailment of the religious freedom of individuals and communities is not only a painful experience, but it is above all an attack on man's very dignity, independently of the religion professed or of the concept of the world which these individuals and communities have."

As Moscow clamped down on Poland, declaring martial law in 1981, Reagan and the pope intensified both political maneuvering behind the scenes and their support for the Solidarity movement. In June 1989, when Poland held free and open elections for the first time under communism, the stage was set for dramatic political change. Five months later, the Berlin Wall fell and, along with it, Eastern European communism.

3 **Theology of the Body.** Even before his election as pope in 1978, Karol Wojtyła recognized that the culture had developed a serious misunderstanding of the human person. When he published his first book, *Love and Responsibility*, in 1960, the sexual revolution was not yet in full swing. He intended it as a resource for those who desire to cultivate a correct Christian anthropology, particularly with regard to human sexuality.

The cultural confusion about the purpose of human sexuality led to massive dissent from Pope Saint Paul VI's *Humanae Vitae* among bishops, priests, and laypeople within the Church. Seeking to put that prophetic document in proper context — and to build a base for its understanding — Pope John Paul II launched a series of lectures (130 in all) during his Wednesday general audiences, from September 5, 1979, to November 28, 1984. This series of orations, which came to be known as the Theology of the Body, was the first major teaching of his pontificate — and one of the most significant.

John Paul II's Theology of the Body presents a holistic vision of Christian life rooted in the fact that God created man to experience real love through a free, unconditional, and reciprocal gift of self to the other, culminating in the union of a husband and wife. John Paul's integrated vision of the human person asserted that the human body has a specific meaning, making visible an invisible reality. He taught that the human body is capable of revealing answers to fundamental questions about humans and our lives — and of revealing God. "Man, whom God created male and female, bears the divine image imprinted on his body 'from the beginning,'" he said in a 1980 general audience. "Man and woman constitute two different ways of the human 'being a body' in the unity of that image."

John Paul asserted that the human person "was not created to be solitary but to live in communion with others," wrote American theologian Cardinal Avery Dulles. "By God's design, male and female are complementary. This complementarity comes to its fullest expression in the marital act, which is intrinsically ordered toward procreation — an activity whereby human beings are privileged to participate in the creative action of God. The total self-giving of the partners demands openness to the generation of new life."

Above all, John Paul viewed marital love through the lens of Christ's love for his Bride, the Church. Such love, he said, necessitates sacrifice: "Christ manifests the love with which he has loved her [the Church] by giving himself for her. That love is an image and above all a model of the love which the husband should show to his wife in marriage, when the two are subject to each other 'out of reverence for Christ.'"

This groundbreaking teaching also brings the modern world a more complete understanding of freedom, sexual love, and the relationship between them. In 1999, papal biographer George Weigel predicted how revolutionary this work would become:

> John Paul II's Theology of the Body is emphatically not made for the age of the twenty-second sound bite or for a media environment in which every idea must be labeled "liberal" or "conservative." It may also be the case that the Theology of the Body will be seriously engaged only when John Paul II, a lightning rod of controversy, is gone from the historical stage. These 130 catechetical addresses, taken together, constitute a kind of theological time bomb set to go off, with dramatic consequences, sometime in the third millennium of the Church.

2 **Divine Mercy.** John Paul II's promotion of the Divine Mercy message is one of the most important ways in which he changed the world. The pope and Saint Faustina Kowalska were pivotal players in God's plan to set the stage for Jesus' Second Coming.

Many believe that Divine Mercy is simply a pious devotion. It *is* a pious devotion, but it's much more. Divine Mercy is God's love poured out for mankind during the time before Jesus' return or before our particular judgment at the foot of his throne immediately after our death, whichever comes first. It's Jesus reaching out to each of us personally, calling us to repent *now* because he wants us to spend eternity with him.

Even before he became pope, Wojtyła played a key role in authenticating the Divine Mercy message Jesus had given to Sister Faustina during the 1930s. The young nun had only three years' schooling, so her diary detailing her mystical experiences was written like that of a child. Bad translations were leaked out of communist Poland after her death in 1938, so the Vatican put a prohibition on spreading her writings. As archbishop of Kraków, Wojtyła subjected Faustina's diary to its first scholarly analysis, and he opened her cause for canonization.

In his 1980 papal encyclical, *Dives in Misericordia* ("Rich in Mercy"), John Paul II asked the faithful to plead for God's mercy as the only answer to humanity's tribulations. George Weigel writes, "John Paul II, who said that he felt spiritually 'very near' to Sister Faustina, had been 'thinking about her for a long time' when he began *Dives in Misericordia.*" In 1982, the Holy Father said that God had called him to help spread the message of mercy: "Right from the beginning of my ministry in Saint Peter's See in Rome, I considered [spreading the Divine Mercy] message my special task. Providence has assigned it to me in the present situation of man, the Church, and the world. It could be said that precisely this situation assigned that message to me as my task before God."

Divine Mercy is woven through the entirety of John Paul's

work as pope. "It is truly marvelous how [Faustina's] devotion to the merciful Jesus is spreading in our contemporary world and gaining so many human hearts!" he said at her beatification. "Where, if not in The Divine Mercy, can the world find refuge and the light of hope?" A year later he said, "As people of this restless time of ours, wavering between the emptiness of self-exaltation and the humiliation of despair, we have a greater need than ever for a regenerating experience of mercy."

Jesus made two demands of Faustina: to have an image of him painted as she saw him in her vision and to have the Sunday after Easter dedicated to his mercy. When John Paul canonized her in 2000, he fulfilled the latter demand, declaring that "it is important then that we accept the whole message that comes to us from the word of God on this Second Sunday of Easter, which from now on throughout the Church *will be called 'Divine Mercy Sunday.'*"

That day, he called Faustina "a gift of God for our time," saying that the Divine Mercy message is the "bridge to the third [millennium]. ... By this act [of canonization of Sister Faustina] I intend today to pass this message on to the new millennium. I pass it on to all people, so that they will learn to know ever better the true face of God."

1 **The New Evangelization.** The Church exists to evangelize. The first thing Jesus said at the outset of his public ministry was, "Come and see" (Jn 1:39) — an invitation to follow him. The last thing he said was, "Go therefore and make disciples of all nations" (Mt 28:19). Throughout her two-thousand-year history, the Church has not always been effective at her core mission. She has been distracted, often fixated on temporal matters rather than on the work entrusted to her by her founder, Jesus Christ. Pope John Paul II recognized that reality and set out to bring Jesus to the world.

John Paul also recognized that changing times and cultures called for new ways of bringing the Gospel to the world — in particular to the world that has already heard the Gospel and forgotten or discarded it. Thus, he began a new program of evangelization. To be clear, what John Paul taught wasn't really new. In fact, he was building on the council's work and on that of his predecessors. In 1975, ten years after Vatican II's close, Paul VI stated that the Church "exists in order to evangelize, that is to say, in order to preach and teach, to be the channel of the gift of grace, to reconcile sinners with God, and to perpetuate Christ's sacrifice in the Mass."

Although John Paul first officially called for a "New Evangelization" in his 1990 encyclical *Redemptoris Missio* (The Mission of the Redeemer), he was already talking about it seven years earlier. Noting that it had been nearly five hundred years since Christopher Columbus brought the Gospel to the Americas, he told Latin American bishops in 1983 that "the commemoration of the half millennium of evangelization will gain its full energy if it is a commitment, not to re-evangelize but to a New Evangelization, new in its ardor, methods and expression."

He further laid the groundwork for this New Evangelization in 1988, telling the Church that "the present-day phenomenon of secularism is truly serious, not simply as regards the individual, but in some ways, as regards whole communities, as the [Second Vatican] Council has already indicated: 'Growing numbers of people are abandoning religion in practice' (*Gaudium et Spes*, par. 7). At other times I myself have recalled the phenomenon of de-Christianization that strikes longstanding Christian people, and which continually calls for a re-evangelization.'"

John Paul laid out his powerful vision for winning the world for Christ in *Redemptoris Missio* (1990). In it, he listed three settings in which evangelization is necessary: among those who have never heard the Gospel; among existing, vibrant Christian communities; and among Christian communities with ancient roots that "have lost a living sense of the faith, or even no longer consider themselves members of the Church, and live a life far removed from Christ and his Gospel. In this case what is needed is a 'new evangelization' or a 're-evangelization.'"

The pope pulled no punches, saying that it is a *requirement* for every follower of Jesus to evangelize: "God is opening before the Church the horizons of a humanity more fully prepared for the sowing of the Gospel. I sense that the moment has come to commit all of the Church's energies to a new evangelization and to the mission *ad gentes* [to the nations]. No believer in Christ, no institution of the Church can avoid this supreme duty: to proclaim Christ to all peoples."

When a pope says with unwavering conviction that the Church must commit all of her energies to an initiative, the faithful *must* sit up and take note. If the Catholic Church were a corporation, evangelization would be core to its mission statement. Without doing the work of bringing souls to Christ, the Church is lost. Without doing the work of evangelization, Christians are lost. After all, faith without works is dead (see Jas 2:17). The Holy Father put his emphasis on personal holiness and evangelization every day of his life. We are called to do the same. Pope Saint John Paul II, pray for us!

Acknowledgments

Just a quick thank you to those who made this book possible. First, the Marians of the Immaculate Conception who helped school me in Mary, Mercy, and John Paul II — notably Father Seraphim Michalenko, MIC; †Father Walter Pelczynski, MIC; Brother Andrew Maczynski, MIC; Father Jan Rokosz, MIC; Father Joseph Roesch, MIC; †Father Mark Garrow, MIC; Father Don Calloway, MIC; and Father Kazimierz Chwalek, MIC. Thanks as well to Vinny Flynn; Jason Free; Dave Came; Fran Bourdon; †Father George Kosicki, CSB*; and Richard Cervera (for pulling the winning ticket that got me to Rome).

I also owe a debt of gratitude to my parents, George and Theresa Novecosky, and to my eight siblings for their love and support. A profound thanks to George Weigel for helping make John Paul II accessible and understandable to junior scholars like me. Also to Paul Kengor for writing the foreword to this book and for his friendship. Finally, I will be forever indebted to my extraordinary wife, Michele, and our children for their love, prayers, and encouragement.

* † Indicates individual is deceased

Notes

Introduction

"… such as the world could never give."

> John Paul II, "Address to the Young People of New Orleans," accessed January 23, 2020, Vatican.va, par. 10.

100. Religious Freedom

"… He is the image and likeness of God himself."

> Karol Wojtyła, "Homily at Consecration of Nowa Huta Parish," accessed January 23, 2020, quoted in https://www.catholicnewsagency.com/news/john-paul-ii-a-man-indispensable-to-the-fall-of-the-soviet-union

"… to *impose an answer* to the mystery of man."

> John Paul II, "Address to the Fiftieth General Assembly of the United Nations Organization," accessed January 23, 2020, Vatican.va, par. 10.

"'… it is impossible to make someone believe.'"

> Paul Kengor, *A Pope and a President: John Paul II, Ronald Reagan, and the Extraordinary Untold Story of the 20th Century* (Wilmington, DE: ISI Books, 2017), 488.

99. Dying with Dignity

"… the person whose suffering we cannot bear."

> John Paul II, *Evangelium Vitae*, accessed January 23, 2020, Vatican.va, par. 66

98. The Shroud of Turin

"… mirror of the Gospel."

> John Paul II, "Address at Turin," accessed January 23, 2020, Vatican.va, par. 3.

"…the questions connected with this Sheet."

> Ibid., par. 2.

"…to his reason and his life."

> Ibid.

"… every temptation to despair."

> Ibid., par. 8.

"… love *speaks to every human heart.*"

> John Paul II, "Angelus, August 13, 2000," accessed January 23, 2020, Vatican.va, par. 1.

97. Friendship with Padre Pio

"… his most painful and bloody wound."

> Mary O'Regan, "John Paul II Was the Only Pope Who Padre Pio Entrusted with the Most Private Detail of His Stigmata," *Catholic Herald*, April 25, 2014, https:// catholicherald.co.uk/commentandblogs/2014/04/25 /john-paul-ii-was-the-only-pope-who-padre-pio -entrusted-with-the-most-private-detail-of-his -stigmata/.

"… healed before entering the operating room."

> Letter from Archbishop Wojtyła to Padre Pio, quoted in "John Paul II and Padre Pio: Two Great Friends," *Michael Journal*, April 30, 2002, https:// www.michaeljournal.org/articles/roman-catholic -church/item/john-paul-ii-and-padre-pio-two -great-friends.

"… a key that opens the heart of God."

> John Paul II, "Homily at the Canonization of St Pio of Pietrelcina," accessed January 23, 2020, Vatican.va, par. 4.

96. Visits to the United States

"... — as archbishop of Kraków."

"Join the Karol Wojtyla Society: Orchard Lake Planned Giving," Orchard Lake Schools, Michigan, accessed November 20, 2019, http://www.orchardlakeschools .com/NEWols/pages/Giving_PlannedGiving.html.

"... having the right to do what we ought."

John Paul II, "Homily at Oriole Park at Camden Yards, Baltimore," accessed January 23, 2020, Vatican.va, par. 7.

"... with liberty and justice for all."

Francis X. Clines, "Pope Ends U.S. Visit with Capital Mass Affirming Doctrine," *New York Times*, October 8, 1979.

"... the warm hospitality of the American people."

John Paul II, "Address at Logan Airport, Boston," accessed January 23, 2020, Vatican.va.

95. End Times

... to prepare the world for his final coming.

Maria Faustina Kowalska, *Diary: Divine Mercy in My Soul* (Stockbridge, MA: Marian Press, 2005), 429.

"... critical phase of the history of the Church."

John Paul II, *Dives in Misericordia*, accessed January 23, 2020, Vatican.va, par. 15.

"... between Christ and the antichrist."

Keith Fournier, "Remembering Saint John Paul II and His Prophetic Warning to the U.S.," Catholic Online, October 22, 2019, https://www.catholic.org/news /national/story.php?id=57376.

"... assiduous in praying the Rosary."

John Paul II, Testimony in Fulda, Germany, 1980, published in the October 1981 issue of *Stimme des Glaubens*, https://www.scribd.com/document/147591704 /Published-Testimony-Pope-John-Paul-II-in -Fulda-Germany-1980.

94. Admiration for Archbishop Fulton Sheen

"… in dissecting atheistic communism."

> Paul Kengor, "A Pope, a President and a Bishop: John Paul II, Ronald Reagan and Fulton Sheen," *National Catholic Register*, August 3, 2017, http://www.ncregister.com/daily-news/a-pope-a-president -and-a-bishop-john-paul-ii-ronald-reagan-and-fulton -sheen.

… his approach to speaking in English.

> Patrick Coffin, "The Miracle of Fulton Sheen — Bonnie Engstrom," accessed January 23, 2020, PCM, https://www.patrickcoffin.media/the-miracle-of-fulton -sheen/.

"… loyal son of the Church."

> Kengor, "A Pope, a President and a Bishop."

93. Relations with Islam

… he kissed the Quran in 1999.

> Robert Moynihan, "Letter #8 The Meaning of a Kiss," *Inside the Vatican*, April 15, 2011, https://insidethevatican.com/news/newsflash/letter-8-the -meaning-of-a-kiss/.

"… and to offer each other forgiveness."

> John Paul II, "Address to Muslim Leaders, Omayyad Great Mosque, Damascus," accessed January 23, 2020, Vatican.va, par. 4.

"… is very distant from Christianity."

> John Paul II, *Crossing the Threshold of Hope* (New York: Alfred A. Knopf, 1994), 92–93.

"… no room for hatred, discrimination or violence."

> John Paul II, "Angelus, Pastoral Visit in Kazakhstan, September 23, 2001," accessed January 23, 2020, Vatican.va.

92. World Peace

"… his more than twenty-six-year pontificate."

> Heinz-Gerhard Justenhoven, "The Peace Ethics of Pope John Paul II," *University of St. Thomas Law Journal* 3, no. 1 (Summer 2005): 110, https://ir.stthomas.edu/cgi /viewcontent.cgi?article=1076&context=ustlj.

"… and violence does not."

> John Paul II, "Homily at Holy Mass in Drogheda," accessed January 23, 2020, Vatican.va, par. 14.

"… It is always a defeat for humanity."

> John Paul II, "Address to the Diplomatic Corps (January 13, 2003)," accessed January 23, 2020, Vatican.va, par. 4.

"… Peace will be the last word of history."

> John Paul II, "Message for the Celebration of the Day of Peace, January 1, 1979," accessed January 23, 2020, Vatican.va, ch. III.

91. Impact on Poland

"… placed on her head by John Paul II."

> Alex Tate, "John Paul II: 'Poland's Pope,'" Georgetown University Berkley Center, March 15, 2012, https:// berkleycenter.georgetown.edu/posts/john-paul-ii -poland-s-pope.

"… at a time of huge and deep divisions."

> "John Paul II Awoke Solidarity, Desire for Freedom in Poles — PM," *The First News*, June 3, 2019, https://www .thefirstnews.com/article/john-paul-ii-awoke -solidarity-desire-for-freedom-in-poles---pm-6180.

90. "Letter to Artists"

"… to the universal desire for redemption."

> John Paul II, "Letter to Artists," accessed January 23, 2020, Vatican.va, par. 10.

"... and of humanity as a whole."
> Ibid., par. 3.

"... to make of it a work of art, a masterpiece."
> Ibid., par. 2.

"... of the Gospel parable of the talents."
> Ibid., par. 3.

"artistic vocation in the service of beauty."
> Ibid.

"... of some possible profit for themselves."
> Ibid., par. 4.

89. Theater

"... and for the theater."
> John Paul II, *Gift and Mystery* (New York: Image, April 20, 1999), 6.

"... To the whole of reality?"
> George Weigel, *Witness to Hope: The Biography of Pope John Paul II, 1920–2005* (New York: HarperCollins, 2005), 38.

"... into the mystery of man."
> John Paul II, "Letter to Artists," par. 14.

88. Poetry

"... and the mystical experience."
> Weigel, *Witness to Hope*, 117.

"... fruits of man's spirit."
> John Paul II, "Address to the 34th General Assembly of the United Nations," accessed January 23, 2020, Vatican.va, par. 14.

87. Friendship with Cardinal Stefan Wyszyński

"... into the next millennium."
> Alessandra Stanley, "Pontiff Ushers in the Millennium Holy Year," *South Florida Sun Sentinel*, December 25, 1999, https://www.sun-sentinel.com/news/fl-xpm

-1999-12-25-9912260198-story.html.

86. Solidarity (*Solidarność*) Trade Union

"… as an initiator of an ethical movement."

> Paweł Skibiński, "The Pope Who Changed Poland," interview by Karolina Kowalska, October 16, 2018, https://poland.pl/history/history-poland/pope-changed-poland/.

… roughly $50 million to Solidarity's efforts.

> Tony Judt, *Postwar: A History of Europe since 1945* (New York: Penguin Books, 2005), 589.

"… as an alternative to a higher being."

> Kenneth S. Zagacki, "Pope John Paul II and the Crusade against Communism: A Case Study in Secular and Sacred Time," *Rhetoric & Public Affairs* 4:4 (2001), 689–710.

"… from East Germany to Bulgaria."

> Richard Bernstein, "Pope Helped Bring Poland Its Freedom," *New York Times*, April 6, 2005, https://www.nytimes.com/2005/04/06/world/europe/pope-helped-bring-poland-its-freedom.html.

84. Surviving Assassination

… and nearly five months of convalescence.

> Henry Tanner, "Pope Out of Hospital, Back at Vatican," *New York Times*, August 15, 1981, https://www.nytimes.com/1981/08/15/world/pope-out-of-hospital-back-at-vatican.html.

83. Forgiving Mehmet Ali Ağca

… are possible in a fallen world.

> "Pope John Paul II Meets with Mehmet Agca, the Man Who Attempted to Assassinate Him, 1983," Rare Historical Photos, May 3, 2016, https://rarehistoricalphotos.com/pope-john-paul-mehmet-agca-1983/.

"… we are all his children in Jesus Christ."

> Henry Kamm, "Pope Meets in Jail with His Attacker," *New York Times*, December 28, 1983, https://www.nytimes.com/1983/12/28/world/pope-meets-in-jail-with-his-attacker.html.

… was released from jail in 2010.

> Editorial, "Pardon for the Pope's Attacker," *New York Times*, June 16, 2000, https://www.nytimes.com/2000/06/16/opinion/pardon-for-the-pope-s-attacker.html.

82. Friendship with Ronald Reagan

… and both were athletes and talented actors.

> Kengor, *A Pope and a President.*

"… an American representative to the Vatican."

> Inés San Martín, "Those 29 Times Presidents and Popes Have Intersected," *Crux*, May 19, 2017, https://cruxnow.com/church-in-the-usa/2017/05/19/29-times-presidents-popes-intersected/.

"… he's still my best friend."

> Paul Kengor, "A Pope and a President: John Paul II, Ronald Reagan, and the Collapse of Communism," *Providence* no. 7 (Spring 2017): 35–36, https://providencemag.com/2017/09/pope-president-john-paul-ii-ronald-reagan-collapse-communism/.

81. Friendship with Mother Teresa

"… the hunger for freedom."

> Ines A. Murzaku, "The Footsteps of Saints: Mother Teresa and John Paul II," *The Catholic Thing*, September 3, 2016, https://www.thecatholicthing.org/2016/09/03/the-footsteps-of-saints-mother-teresa-and-john-paul-ii/.

"'… a house built on courage and faith.'"

> John Paul II, quoted in ibid.

"… and follow her example."

John Paul II, "Homily at the Beatification of Mother Teresa of Calcutta," accessed January 23, 2020, Vatican.va, par. 6.

80. Visits to Mexico

"… an almost smothering embrace."

Stanisław Dziwisz, *A Life with Karol: My Forty-Year Friendship with the Man Who Became Pope* (New York: Doubleday, 2008), 75–76.

"… instrument for formation and action."

John Paul II, "Address to the Third General Conference of the Latin American Episcopate at Puebla, Mexico," accessed January 23, 2020, Vatican.va, III.7.

… of Marxism.

George Weigel, *The End and the Beginning: Pope John Paul II — The Victory of Freedom, the Last Years, the Legacy* (New York: Doubleday, 2010), 104.

"… were in coats and ties)."

Inés San Martín, "The Land of Mariachis and Tequila Is a Favorite Papal Destination," *Crux*, February 13, 2016, https://cruxnow.com/church/2016/02/13 /the-land-of-mariachis-and-tequila-is-a-favorite -papal-destination/.

"… 'I feel I am a Mexican Pope.'"

Benedict XVI, "Address in Front of Miraflores College," accessed January 23, 2020, Vatican.va.

79. Our Lady of Guadalupe

"… most profound devotion to you."

John Paul II, "Homily at the Basilica of Guadalupe, Mexico," accessed January 23, 2020, Vatican.va, par. 2.

"… which enriches the whole Church."

John Paul II, "Address at the Inauguration of the Virgin of Guadalupe Chapel in the Vatican Crypt," accessed

January 23, 2020, available in Spanish at Vatican.va.

"... American sons and daughters!"

> John Paul II, "Homily at the Basilica of Our Lady of Guadalupe, Mexico City," accessed January 23, 2020, Vatican.va, par. 9.

78. Social Justice

"... among individuals, families and groups."

> John Paul II, "Audience (July 28, 1993)," accessed January 23, 2020, par. 2, available in French, Italian, and Spanish at Vatican.va.

"... in view of a new world order."

> John Paul II, *Evangelium Vitae*, par. 5.

77. Denunciation of Liberation Theology

"... by no Christianity worthy of the name."

> Michael Novak, "The Case against Liberation Theology," *New York Times Magazine*, October 21, 1984, 51, https://www.nytimes.com/1984/10/21/magazine/the-case-against-liberation-theology.html.

"... does not tally with the Church's catechesis."

> John Paul II, "Address to the Third General Conference of the Latin American Episcopate at Puebla, Mexico," accessed January 23, 2020, Vatican.va, I.4.

"... liberation from sin and the Evil One."

> Ibid., III.6.

"... begets violence and degrades man."

> Congregation for the Doctrine of the Faith, "Instruction on Certain Aspects of the 'Theology of Liberation,'" accessed January 23, 2020, Vatican.va, par. 7.

76. Stand against Socialism

"... enable them to share in development."

> John Paul II, *Centesimus Annus*, accessed January 23, 2020, Vatican.va, par. 35.

"... whose decisions build the social order."

Ibid., par. 13.

"... solution to the 'question of the working class.'"

Ibid., par. 12.

75. Meeting with Dictators

"... *may the world open itself up to Cuba.*"

John Paul II, "Welcome Ceremony Address, Apostolic Journey to Cuba," accessed January 23, 2020, Vatican.va, par. 5.

"... have not been fulfilled."

Tom Gjelten, "Previous Papal Visits Changed Little, but Cubans Hopeful for Pope Francis," NPR, September 12, 2015, https://www.npr.org/sections /parallels/2015/09/11/439507567/previous-papal-visits -changed-little-but-cubans-hopeful-for-pope-francis.

"They chose the latter option."

Filip Mazurczak, "Remembering Saint John Paul II's Controversial 1987 Pilgrimage to Chile," Catholic World Report, January 14, 2018, https:// www.catholicworldreport.com/2018/01/14 /remembering-st-john-paul-iis-controversial-1987 -pilgrimage-to-chile/.

74. The Popemobile

... by the German car manufacturer in 1930.

Danny Lewis, "A Brief History of the Popemobile," *SmartNews*, September 17, 2015, https:// www.smithsonianmag.com/smart-news/short -history-popemobile-180956657.

... so the pope could be seen at night.

Kristen Hall-Geisler, "Heaven on Wheels: 7 Super Cool Popemobiles," *Mental Floss*, September 23, 2015, http:// mentalfloss.com/article/49259/heaven-wheels-7 -super-cool-popemobiles.

73. Visits to Canada

... Toronto, Hamilton, London, Yellowknife, and Saint Catharines.

> Weigel, *Witness to Hope,* 222.

"... ready to work for a new world."

> John Paul II, "Farewell Ceremony Address at Uplands Military Airport, Ottawa," accessed January 23, 2020, Vatican.va, par. 4.

"... will walk that path with you."

> John Paul II, "Address to the Native Peoples of Canada," accessed January 23, 2020, Vatican.va, par. 6.

"... words warm our hearts."

> John Paul II, "Address at the Evening Vigil with Young People, 17th World Youth Day," accessed January 23, 2020, Vatican.va, pars. 2–3.

72. His Longevity

"... as a special divine gift."

> John Paul II, "Message for Lent 2005," accessed January 23, 2020, Vatican.va, par. 1.

"... to succeed to the throne."

> Gerard Mannion, ed., *The Vision of John Paul II: Assessing His Thought and Influence* (Collegeville, MN: Liturgical Press, 2008), 10.

71. Multilingual Communication

"... when he was tired."

> Caroline Pigozzi, *Pope John Paul II: An Intimate Life: The Pope I Knew So Well* (Paris: Lagardére, 2007).

... Spanish had improved dramatically.

> Sofia Celeste, "Language May Be Key for Next Pope," *Boston Globe,* April 15, 2005, http://archive.boston.com /news/world/europe/articles/2005/04/15 /language_may_be_key_for_next_pope/.

… greetings in sixty-two languages.

> Weigel, *The End and the Beginning*, 353.

70. His Productivity

"… was his constant prayer."

> Weigel, *Witness to Hope*, 201.

"… in spheres that include human rights."

> John Paul II, *Laborem Exercens*, accessed January 23, 2020, Vatican.va, pars. 9, 11.

69. Prayer

"… the source of our true light, Jesus himself."

> John Paul II, "Address to the Young People at the Kiel Center," accessed January 23, 2020, Vatican.va, par. II.4.

68. Education

… to include skiing and kayaking trips.

> Alison Behnke, *Pope John Paul II* (Minneapolis: Twenty-First Century Books, 2006), 48.

"… of helping to form Christ in the lives of others."

> John Paul II, "Message to the National Catholic Educational Association of the United States," accessed January 23, 2020, Vatican.va.

"… in your youth groups and Newman Centers."

> John Paul II, "Address to the Young People at the Kiel Center," par. 4.

"… can grasp the truth of things."

> John Paul II, "Address to the Bishops of the Ecclesiastical Regions of Chicago, Indianapolis and Milwaukee (U.S.A.) on Their 'Ad Limina' Visit," accessed January 23, 2020, Vatican.va, par. 3.

67. Angels

"… In this, we are powerfully helped by the good angels."

> John Paul II, "General Audience, August 20, 1986,"

available in Italian, Spanish, and Portuguese at
Vatican.va, par. 5

"... of people and solicitude for their salvation."

Ibid., par. 6

"... still alive and active in the world."

John Paul II, "Address at Monte Sant'Angelo," accessed
January 23, 2020, available in Italian at
Vatican.va, par. 3.

66. Teaching on Homosexuality

"... is a morally acceptable option. It is not."

Congregation for the Doctrine of the Faith, "Letter to
the Bishops of the Catholic Church on the Pastoral Care
of Homosexual Persons," accessed January 23, 2020,
Vatican.va, par. 3.

"... against the family and man."

John Paul II, *Memory and Identity: Personal Reflections*
(Città del Vaticano: Libreria Editrice Vaticana, 2005), 11.

65. Christian Unity

"We are brothers."

John Paul II, quoted in "We Are Brothers," *Christianity
Today*, May 24, 2005, https://www.christianitytoday
.com/ct/2005/june/17.28.html.

"... and I consider myself deeply responsible for it."

John Paul II, "Address to the College of Cardinals, June
28, 1985," accessed January 23, 2020, available in Italian
at Vatican.va, par. 10

"... for interreligious dialogue presuppose and signify."

"Pope Says Day of Prayer Was Model," *New York Times*,
December 23, 1986, https://www.nytimes
.com/1986/12/23/world/pope-says-day-of-prayer
-was-model.html.

"... be shaped, as it were, by that concern."

John Paul II, *Ut Unum Sint*, accessed January 23, 2020,

Vatican.va, par. 15.

"... informed that they were mistaken."

Weigel, *Witness to Hope*, 761.

64. Outreach to the Orthodox Churches

"... a real commitment to restoring Christian unity."

Teoctist, quoted in Stephen F. Brown and Khaled
Antolios, *Catholicism & Orthodox Christianity*, 3rd ed.
(New York: Infobase Publishing, 2009), 71.

"... the Churches of the East and the West."

John Paul II, *Ut Unum Sint*, par. 54.

... and the custom a Holy See delegation visiting Istanbul.

Ibid., par. 52.

"... in the quest for a more humane world."

Weigel, *Witness to Hope*, 885.

"... a priority demand of my ministry."

John Paul II, "Angelus Address on the Feast of the Conversion of Saint Paul, January 25, 2004," accessed January 23, 2020, Vatican.va, par. 2.

63. Diplomacy with Russia

"... no such pilgrimage was possible."

Weigel, *Witness to Hope*, 834.

... Polish, German, and Lithuanian extraction.

BBC, "Russia and the Vatican Establish Full Diplomatic
Ties," December 3, 2009, http://news.bbc.co.uk/2/hi
/europe/8394079.stm.

... in the resumption of dialogue.

Zenit, "Meeting with Alexy II Viewed as a Step For-
ward," February 23, 2004, https://zenit.org/articles
/meeting-with-alexy-ii-viewed-as-a-step-forward/.

62. Visit to the United Kingdom

... Britain's first ambassador to the Holy See.

David Kerr, "UK Celebrates 30 Years of Diplomacy

with Vatican," Catholic News Agency, March 30, 2012, https://www.catholicnewsagency.com/news/uk -celebrates-30-years-of-diplomacy-with-vatican.

61. Speeches at the United Nations

"... and the pursuit of peace."

Weigel, *Witness to Hope*, 343–44.

"*... their full rights under any political regime or system.*"

John Paul II, "Address to the 34th General Assembly of the United Nations," par. 19.

"... for a new springtime of the human spirit."

John Paul II, "Address to the Fiftieth General Assembly of the United Nations," accessed January 23, 2020, Vatican.va, par. 18.

60. Inspiring Vocations

"John Paul II priests."

See Timothy M. Dolan, "John Paul II Priests," Catholic Education Resource Center, May 1, 2011, https://www. catholiceducation.org/en/faith-and-character /faith-and-character/john-paul-ii-priests.html; Laurie Goodstein, "Catholics in America: A Restive People," *New York Times*, April 3, 2005, https://www.nytimes .com/2005/04/03/weekinreview/catholics-in -america-a-restive-people.html.

"... does not cease to carry out."

John Paul II, "Message for the 41st World Day of Prayer for Vocations," accessed January 23, 2020, Vatican.va, par. 3.

"... and to the consecrated life."

John Paul II, "Letter to Priests for Holy Thursday 2004," accessed January 23, 2020, Vatican.va, par. 4.

"... the priesthood and religious life."

Jonathan Luxmoore, "'Evangelical Moment': World Youth Day Often Fosters Vocations," *Crux*, August 2, 2016, https://cruxnow.com/cns/2016/08/02

/evangelical-moment-world-youth-day-often
-fosters-vocations/.

"… They were tired of living in doubt and fear."

Dolan, "John Paul II Priests."

"… teacher and mother."

John Paul II, *Pastores Dabo Vobis*, accessed January 23, 2020, Vatican.va, par. 41.

59. Intervening with the Jesuits

"… who enjoy the Vatican's confidence."

"Religion: John Paul Takes On the Jesuits," *Time*, November 9, 1981.

"… or even composed by the students."

James Hitchcock, *The Pope and the Jesuits: John Paul II and the New Order in the Catholic Church*, (New York: National Committee of Catholic Laymen, 1984), 40.

… for spreading confusion in the Church.

See John Paul II, "Speech to Representatives of the Company of Jesus," accessed January 23, 2020, available in French, Italian, Spanish, and Portuguese at Vatican.va.

"… movements in Guatemala and El Salvador."

Paul Hofmann, "The Jesuits," *New York Times Magazine*, February 14, 1982, 24, https://www.nytimes.com/1982/02/14/magazine/the-jesuits.html.

"… years of experimentation and innovation."

Austen Ivereigh, *The Great Reformer: Francis and the Making of a Radical Pope* (New York: Henry Holt, 2014), 174.

58. Defending Copernicus

"… to inspire service 'to our brothers.'"

Debora MacKenzie, "Copernicus Earns Papal Blessing," *New Scientist*, October 30, 1993, https://www.newscientist.com/article/mg14018970-900-copernicus-earns-papal-blessing/.

57. Revisiting Galileo

"… from men and Church organizations."

John Paul II, "Address for the Commemoration of the Birth of Albert Einstein," accessed January 23, 2020, http://www.casinapioiv.va/content/accademia/en /magisterium/johnpaulii/10november1979.html, par. 6.

"… were simply incompatible."

Weigel, *The End and the Beginning*, 461.

"… literal meaning of Sacred Scripture."

John Paul II, "Address to the Pontifical Academy of Sciences, October 31, 1992," accessed January 23, 2020, http://www.accademiascienze.va/content /accademia/en/magisterium/johnpaulii/31october1992 .html, pars. 11–12.

56. Faith and Science

"… in which both can flourish."

John Paul II, "Letter to Reverend George V. Coyne, S.J., Director of the Vatican Observatory," accessed January 23, 2020, Vatican.va.

"… I assure all my support."

John Paul II, "Message to the Members of the Plenary Assembly of the Pontifical Academy of Sciences," par. 6.

"… evolution more than a hypothesis."

John Paul II, "Message to the Members of the Plenary Assembly of the Pontifical Academy of Sciences, October 22, 1996," accessed January 23, 2020, http://www .accademiascienze.va/content/accademia/en /magisterium/johnpaulii/22october1996.html, par. 4.

"… to grow, in humanity."

John Paul II, "Address to the Pontifical Academy of Sciences, November 13, 2000," accessed January 23, 2020, Vatican.va, par. 3.

55. Anticipating Climate Change

"... to destroy it for use by future generations."

> John Paul II, "Homily at Mass for the Rural Workers, Laguna Seca, California," accessed January 23, 2020, Vatican.va, par. 6.

"... made the air unbreathable."

> John Paul II, "General Audience, January 17, 2001," Vatican.va, par. 3.

"... for others and dishonesty."

> John Paul II, "Message for the Celebration of the World Day of Peace, January 1, 1990," accessed January 23, 2020, Vatican.va, par. 1.

54. Defense of Agriculture

"... is of *fundamental importance.*"

> John Paul II, *Laborem Exercens*, par. 21.

... a whopping 350,000 pilgrims.

> "Saint Pope John Paul II Visit," Living History Farms, accessed November 20, 2019, https://www.lhf.org /aboutus/saint-pope-john-paul-ii-visit/.

"... it is Christ alone who is the bread of life."

> John Paul II, "Homily at Mass at the Living History Farms," accessed January 23, 2020, Vatican.va, pars. 1, 3.

"... and the future of the earth."

> John Paul II, "Address at the Jubilee of the Agricultural World," accessed January 23, 2020, Vatican.va, pars. 5, 4.

53. Guiding Economic Policy

"... unbridled capitalism."

> John Paul II, "Address to the Participants in the Colloquium on 'Capitalism and Ethics,'" accessed January 23, 2020, Vatican.va, par. 2.

"... her ministry in the world."

> John Paul II, *Sollicitudo Rei Socialis*, accessed January 23, 2020, Vatican.va, par. 41.

"… economic growth of all humanity."

> John Paul II, *Centesimus Annus*, par. 28.

… to form unions and to strike.

> John Paul II, *Laborem Exercens*, par. 20.

"… but in his success as a pastor."

> Roberto Suro, "John Paul's Economics of Compassion," *New York Times*, September 7, 1986, https://www.nytimes.com/1986/09/07/business/john-paul-s-economics-of-compassion.html.

52. Addressing Poverty

"… like guests at your family table."

> John Paul II, "Homily at Mass at Yankee Stadium," accessed January 23, 2020, Vatican.va, par. 4.

"… and services originally intended for all."

> John Paul II, *Sollicitudo Rei Socialis*, par. 28.

"… from this world of poverty"

> John Paul II, *Novo Millennio Ineunte*, accessed January 23, 2020, Vatican.va, par. 50.

51. Visit to Cuba

"…*may the world open itself up to Cuba.*"

> John Paul II, "Welcome Ceremony Address, Apostolic Journey to Cuba," accessed January 23, 2020, Vatican.va, par. 5.

… in their children's lives.

> Celestine Bohlen, "The Pope in Cuba: The Overview; Pope Challenges Cuba on Abortion and on Education," *New York Times*, January 23, 1998, https://www.nytimes.com/1998/01/23/world/the-pope-in-cuba-the-overview-pope-challenges-cuba-on-abortion-and-on-education.html.

"… to be the protagonists of their destiny."

> Weigel, *Witness to Hope*, 791–92.

... a public holiday ever since.
> "That Time JPII Changed Fidel Castro's Mind about Christmas," Catholic News Agency, December 3, 2016, https://www.catholicnewsagency.com/news /that-time-jpii-changed-fidel-castros-mind -about-christmas-18580.

50. "Be Not Afraid!"

"... He alone knows it."
> John Paul II, "Homily for the Inauguration of His Pontificate," accessed January 23, 2020, Vatican.va, par. 5.

"... This is no time to be ashamed of the Gospel."
> John Paul II, "Homily at the 8th World Youth Day," accessed January 23, 2020, Vatican.va, par. 6.

"... who are determined to enter it."
> John Paul II, "Message to Youth Meeting in Santiago de Compostela," accessed January 23, 2020, Vatican.va, par. 3.

"... *which man could or should fear.*"
> John Paul II, *Crossing the Threshold of Hope*, 218–19.

49. Relations with the Middle East

"... restoring order had been exhausted."
> Weigel, *Witness to Hope*, 621.

48. Visit to Israel

"... vocations as Christians and as Jews."
> John Paul II, "Address on the Occasion of the Colloquium on the Conciliar Declaration," accessed January 23, 2020, Vatican.va.

"... at any time and in any place."
> John Paul II, "Speech during His Visit to the Yad Vashem Museum," accessed January 23, 2020, Vatican.va, par. 3.

"… of God's troops on earth."

> Uri Geller, "Saints Alive! How Can Vatican Beatify Pius IX?" UriGeller.com, July 7, 2000, https://www.urigeller .com/this-weeks-uri-geller-jewish-telegraph-column /the-jewish-telegraph-april-28-to-octover-27-2000 /saints-alive-how-can-vatican-beatify-pius-ix/.

47. Visits to Africa

"… to bring succor to a troubled continent."

> "Africa Needs Saint John Paul II Now More Than Ever," *Crux*, April 7, 2016, https://cruxnow.com /church/2016/04/07/africa-needs-st-john-paul -ii-now-more-than-ever/.

"… rites of purification and expiation."

> John Paul II, *Ecclesia in Africa*, accessed January 23, 2020, Vatican.va, par. 42.

46. Love of Italy

"… we have a Bishop of Rome!"

> "Pope John Paul II," *People*, December 25, 1978, https:// people.com/archive/pope-john-paul-ii-vol-10-no-26/.

"… with the evangelical message."

> John Paul II, "Address to the Italian Youth," accessed January 23, 2020, Vatican.va, par. 3.

45. Affirming Natural Law

"… reflects a set of moral aspirations."

> John F. Coverdale, "The Legacy of John Paul II to Lawyers," *Seton Hall Law Review* 36:1 (2005), 1.

"… that is always a freeing truth."

> John Paul II, "Address to the Prelate Auditors, Officials, and Advocates of the Tribunal of the Roman Rota," accessed January 23, 2020, Vatican.va, par. 4.

"… every innocent human being."

> John Paul II, *Evangelium Vitae*, para. 71.

"… understandings of the human condition."

> Coverdale, "Legacy of John Paul II," 43.

44. Consecrated Women

… to protest the pope's remarks.

> Marjorie Hyer and Megan Rosenfeld, "A Challenge from Nuns," *Washington Post*, October 8, 1979, https://www.washingtonpost.com/archive/politics/1979/10/08/a-challenge-from-nuns/55441365-443c-4349-9928-247665173d2a/.

"… and very life of the Church."

> John Paul II, "Address to Women Religious," accessed January 23, 2020, Vatican.va, introduction.

"… by all the Church's faithful."

> John Paul II, *Ordinatio Sacerdotalis*, accessed January 23, 2020, Vatican.va, par. 4.

"… of their relationship with the Lord."

> John Paul II, *Vita Consecrata*, accessed January 23, 2020, Vatican.va, pars. 25, 34.

43. Elevation of Women

"… in the midst of all peoples and nations."

> John Paul II, *Mulieris Dignitatem*, accessed January 23, 2020, Vatican.va, par. 31.

"… according to God's plan and in his love."

> John Paul II, "Letter to Women," accessed January 23, 2020, Vatican.va, par. 3.

42. Teaching on Sports

… and skiing with his inner circle of priests.

> Dziwisz, *A Life with Karol*, 81–82.

"… to the work that he calls you to do!"

> John Paul II, "Address to the Young People at the Kiel Center," par. 2.

"… loyalty, perseverance, friendship, sharing and solidarity."
> John Paul II, "Homily for the Jubilee of Sports People," accessed January 23, 2020, Vatican.va, par. 2.

"… it is the encounter with Christ."
> John Paul II, "Angelus on the World Day of Peace, January 1, 2000," accessed January 23, 2020, Vatican.va, par. 3.

41. The Mystery of Suffering

… intense prayer life and love for Christ.
> Dziwisz, *A Life with Karol*, 248.

"… the meaning of all that is human."
> John Paul II, "Meeting with the Sick and Suffering, Shrine of Lazarus, El Rincón," accessed January 23, 2020, Vatican.va, par. 3.

"… precisely in this weakness and emptying of self."
> John Paul II, *Salvifici Doloris*, accessed January 23, 2020, Vatican.va, par. 23.

"… especially those who suffer."
> Ibid., par. 29.

40. Response to the Sexual Abuse Crisis

… from the 1950s through the 1980s.
> Matthew E. Bunson, interview with Father Paul Sullins, "Is Catholic Clergy Sex Abuse Related to Homosexual Priests?" *National Catholic Register*, November 2, 2018, http://www.ncregister.com /daily-news/is-catholic-clergy-sex-abuse-related-to -homosexual-priests.

… understood the depth and breadth of the situation.
> Joaquin Navarro-Valls, quoted in Catholic News Service, "JPII's Record on Sex Abuse: Spokesman, biographer discuss how John Paul handled the crisis," *America*, April 25, 2014, https://www.americamagazine.org/issue /jpiis-record-sex-abuse.

"... to the renewal of marriage and family life."

> John Paul II, "Address to the Cardinals of the United States, April 23, 2002," accessed November 21, 2019, Vatican.va, par. 3.

"... caused such suffering and scandal to the young."

> Ibid., par. 1.

"... I don't think he has a vocation to the priesthood."

> Cardinal Francis George, quoted in Julia Lieblich, "'An appalling sin,' pope says," *Chicago Tribune*, April 24, 2002, https://www.chicagotribune.com/news/ct-xpm-2002-04-24-0204240328-story.html.

"... over the next 26 and a half years."

> George Weigel, quoted in "JPII's Record on Sex Abuse," *America*.

39. Outreach to Children

"... and able to live in peace."

> John Paul II, "Letter to Children in the Year of the Family," accessed January 23, 2020, Vatican.va.

"... joyful enthusiasm and hope."

> John Paul II, "Message for the XXIX World Day of Peace," accessed January 23, 2020, Vatican.va, par. 7.

"... set the world ablaze with love!"

> John Paul II, "The Pope to the Children," accessed January 23, 2020, Vatican.va, par. 2.

38. Love of the Circus

"... friendship among people, nothing more."

> Andreas Widmer, *The Pope and the CEO: John Paul II's Leadership Lessons to a Young Swiss Guard* (Steubenville, OH: Emmaus Road Publishing, 2001).

... jacket embroidered with his name.

> Matt Sedensky, "Priest to Circus Workers Relishes Road Mission," *New York Times*, August 21, 2001, https://www.nytimes.com/2001/08/21/us/priest-to-circus

-workers-relishes-road-mission.html.

"... and also with animals."

John Paul II, "Address to Participants in the Sixth International Meeting for the Pastoral Care of Circus and Traveling Show People," accessed January 23, 2020, available in French at Vatican.va, par. 3.

"... to building a universal brotherhood."

John Paul II, "Address to the Circus and Fairground Artists Taking Part in Their Seventh International Congress," accessed January 23, 2020, Vatican.va, par. 3.

37. Response to Medjugorje

"... Is this not perhaps a miracle of God?"

Antonio Gaspari, "Medjugorje Deception or Miracle?" *Inside the Vatican*, November 1996.

"... was able to unleash."

Stanisław Dziwisz, "Will Pope Saint John Paul II Influence the Papal Pronouncement on Medjugorje?," interview by Gian Franco Svidercoschi, *Aleteia*, July 16, 2015, https://aleteia.org/2015/07/16/will-pope-st-john-paul-ii-influence-the-papal-pronouncement-on-medjugorje/.

36. Our Lady of Częstochowa

"... I had whispered *Totus tuus* in prayer"

John Paul II, "Homily at Jasna Góra," accessed January 23, 2020, Vatican.va, par. 2.

"... is about to draw to a close."

"Act of Consecration to the Mother of God" in ibid.

35. Care for the Swiss Guard

"... both on and off duty."

John Paul II, "Address to the Pontifical Swiss Guard," accessed January 23, 2020, Vatican.va, par. 4.

"... to blend into the background as he passed."

Widmer, *The Pope and the CEO*, 75.

34. Care for the Police

… and even wrote a message in an officer's Bible.

> Richard Pérez-Peña, "The Pope's Visit: Pope Blesses the Children of Police Detail," *New York Times*, October 9, 1995, https://www.nytimes.com/1995/10/09/nyregion /the-pope-s-visit-pope-blesses-the-children-of-police -detail.html.

"… need for order and civil peace."

> John Paul II, "Address to a Group of Italian Carabinieri, May 5, 1988," accessed January 23, 2020, available in Italian at Vatican.va, par. 3.

"… with sensitivity and Christian hope."

> John Paul II, "Address to the Representatives of the Catholic Police Officers of England and Wales," accessed January 23, 2020, Vatican.va.

"… what life is all about."

> "1987 Pope John Paul II Visit," Los Angeles Police Department website, accessed November 21, 2019, http:// www.lapdonline.org/history_of_the_lapd/content _basic_view/1131.

33. Honoring Firefighters

"… your great service to your city."

> John Paul II, "Remarks to the Delegation from the New York City Fire Department," accessed January 23, 2020, Vatican.va.

"… will never be praised enough."

> John Paul II, "Address to a Group of Volunteer Firefighters," accessed January 23, 2020, available in Italian at Vatican.va, par. 2.

"… the very figure of Christ, the Savior of men!"

> John Paul II, "Address to the Brigade of Firefighters of Paris," accessed January 23, 2020, available in French and Italian at Vatican.va, par. 2.

… the most famous relic of Christ's Passion.

> See "Pope to Honor Fireman Who Saved the Shroud of Turin," *AP News*, April 13, 1997, https://www.apnews.com/d91234833ed986f68b326acfe39c0681.

32. Concern for Military Personnel

"… over the whole human community."

> Clyde Haberman, "Pope Denounces the Gulf War as 'Darkness,'" *New York Times*, April 1, 1991, https://www.nytimes.com/1991/04/01/world/pope-denounces-the-gulf-war-as-darkness.html.

"… to public opinion even as a peace operator."

> John Paul II, "Address to the Participants in the Third International Conference of Military Orders," accessed January 23, 2020, available in Italian at Vatican.va, par. 4.

"… specific form of pastoral assistance."

> John Paul II, *Spirituali Militum Curae*, accessed January 23, 2020, available in several languages at Vatican.va, introduction.

"… that others will enjoy security and peace."

> John Paul II, "Address to the Third International and Interdenominational Conference of Chief Military Chaplains of Europe and North America," accessed January 23, 2020, Vatican.va, par. 4.

31. Standing Up to the Mafia

… God's wrath in the final Judgment.

> John Paul II, "Homily at Eucharistic Concelebration in the Valley of the Temples, Agrigento," accessed January 23, 2020, Vatican.va.

… gunned down a priest in his own church.

> Weigel, *Witness to Hope*, 677.

"… especially from the power of the Mafia."

> Alan Cowell, "As Pope Visits Sicily, Mafia Sends Gruesome Warning to Priest," *New York Times*, November 6,

1994, https://www.nytimes.com/1994/11/06/world
/as-pope-visits-sicily-mafia-sends-gruesome-warning
-to-priest.html.
"... in a climate of terror, intimidation and death."
John Paul II, "Homily at Holy Mass in Drogheda," accessed January 23, 2020, Vatican.va, par. 9.

30. 1979 Visit to Poland

... young people, families, and large crowds.
Nine Days That Changed the World, DVD, Directed by
Kevin Knoblock. (Washington, DC: Regnery Publishing, 2010)
"... the face of *this land!*"
John Paul II, "Homily at Holy Mass in Victory Square,
Warsaw," accessed January 23, 2020, Vatican.va, pars.
3a, 4.

29. Empowering the Laity

"... courageously identify and denounce evil."
John Paul II, *Christifideles Laici*, accessed January 23,
2020, Vatican.va, par. 14.
"... shares a responsibility for the Church's mission."
Ibid., par. 15.
"... based on personal encounter with Christ."
John Paul II, "Message for the World Congress of Ecclesial Movements and New Communities," accessed
January 23, 2020, par. 2.

28. Faustina Kowalska

"... a faulty Italian translation of her diary."
Weigel, *Witness to Hope*, 387.
"... among our brothers and sisters."
John Paul II, "Homily at the Mass for the Canonization
of Sr. Mary Faustina Kowalska," accessed January 23,
2020, Vatican.va, par. 8.

… the happiest day of his life.

> "The Happiest Day of St. John Paul II's Life," Catholic
> News Agency, October 5, 2016, https://
> www.catholicnewsagency.com/blog/the-happiest-
> day-of-st-john-paul-iis-life.

27. Maximilian Kolbe

"… almost as dear to him as family members."

> Dziwisz, *A Life with Karol*, 176.

"… broke the infernal cycle of hatred."

> Weigel, *Witness to Hope*, 221.

"… not to come here as Pope."

> John Paul II, "Homily at Auschwitz-Bierkenau [sic]," ac-
> cessed January 23, 2020, Vatican.va, par. 2.

… cardinals had voted to the contrary.

> Kenneth L. Woodward, "Making Saints," *Newsweek*,
> November 11, 1990, https://www.newsweek.com
> /making-saints-205696.

"… be proclaimed as a martyr saint."

> John Paul II, "Homily at the Canonization of Maximil-
> ian Maria Kolbe," https://www.piercedhearts.org/jpii
> /jpii_homilies/homilies_1982/oct_10_1982
> _canonization_max_kolbe.htm.

26. Development of Personalism

"… and adequate attitude is love."

> John Paul II, *Love and Responsibility* (San Francisco:
> Ignatius Press, 1983; originally published by William
> Collins Sons, London, and Farrar, Straus and Giroux,
> New York, 1981), 41.

… a disinterested gift of self.

> Paul VI, *Gaudium et Spes*, accessed January 23, 2020,
> Vatican.va, pars. 26, 24.

"… by any human power."

> Avery Dulles, "John Paul II and the Mystery of The Hu-

man Person," *America*, February 2, 2004, https://www
.americamagazine.org/issue/469/article/john-paul
-ii-and-mystery-human-person.
"… to move towards truth and goodness."
John Paul II, *Centesimus Annus*, par. 38.

25. Resistance to Capital Punishment
"… if not practically non-existent."
John Paul II, *Evangelium Vitae*, par. 56.
"… fuel further debate on the issue."
Weigel, *Witness to Hope*, 758.
"… which is both cruel and unnecessary."
John Paul II, "Homily in St. Louis," accessed January 23,
2020, Vatican.va, par. 5.

24. Friendship with Joseph Ratzinger
"… to communicate his knowledge."
Benedict XVI, quoted in E. J. Dionne Jr., "The Pope's
Guardian of Orthodoxy," *New York Times Magazine*,
November 24, 1985, https://www.nytimes
.com/1985/11/24/magazine/the-pope-s-guardian-of
-orthodoxy.html.
… for little more than eighteen months.
Weigel, *Witness to Hope*, 443.
"… the official and the private."
Wlodzimierz Redzioch, *Beside John Paul II: Friends and
Collaborators Speak* (Milan: Ares, 2013).
"… ever more clearly."
Ibid. See also "The Recollections of Pope Benedict," *Inside the Vatican*, May 1, 2014, https://
insidethevatican.com/magazine/people/interview
/recollections-pope-benedict/.

23. Theological Legacy

"… and fulfill their destinies."
>Weigel, *Witness to Hope*, 688.

"… culture, work, and leisure."
>Avery Dulles, "The Theologian," *America*, April 18, 2005, https://www.americamagazine.org/issue/527/article/theologian.

22. Expansion of the College of Cardinals

"… fell to 17 percent by 2005."
>Charles Keenan, "Who Will Be the Next Pope?," History News Network, January 16, 2012, https://historynewsnetwork.org/article/143901.

"… a single common language."
>Weigel, *Witness to Hope*, xiv.

21. The Church in China

"… and constant anxiety of my pontificate."
>John Paul II, quoted in *L'Osservatore Romano*, English weekly edition, February 1, 1982.

"… and for peace in the world."
>John Paul II, "Message to the Participants in the International Conference Commemorating the Fourth Centenary of the Arrival in Beijing of Father Matteo Ricci," accessed January 23, 2020, Vatican.va, par. 6.

"… the herald of the Kingdom of God."
>John Paul II, "Address to the Catholic Communities in Asia, Manila," accessed January 23, 2020, Vatican.va, par. 4.

20. The Dignity of Marriage

"… married life and child rearing."
>Weigel, *Witness to Hope*, 97.

"… wife beating and child abuse."
>Paul Johnson, "Essay: Kitchen Pope, Warrior Pope,"

Time, June 24, 2001, http://content.time.com/time
/magazine/article/0,9171,163504,00.html.
"… a new, rich, humanistic texture."
Weigel, *The End and the Beginning*, 48.

19. Defense of the Family

"… means to create a community."
Wojtyła, *Love and Responsibility*, 242.
"… human development and human happiness!"
John Paul II, "Homily at Aqueduct Racecourse in
Brooklyn, New York," accessed January 23, 2020,
Vatican.va, par. 7.
"… contributing to the renewal of society."
John Paul II, *Familiaris Consortio*, accessed January 23,
2020, Vatican.va, par. 3.
"… values and requirements of the family."
Ibid., par. 86.

18. The Gift of Motherhood

… the highest expression of the feminine genius.
John Paul II, "Letter to Women," par. 10.
"… through the motherhood of the Mother of God"
John Paul II, *Mulieris Dignitatem*, par. 19.
"… what is happening inside her."
Ibid., par. 18.
"… and richness of their femininity."
Ibid., par. 31.

17. Protection for the Unborn

"… akin to religious liberty"
Weigel, *The End and the Beginning*, 440.
"… method of family planning"
John Paul II, "Letter to the Secretary General of the
International Conference on Population and Develop-
ment," accessed January 23, 2020, Vatican.va, par. 5.

"… that is, the right to life"

> John Paul II, "Address to the Bishops of the Polish Episcopal Conference on Their 'Ad Limina' Visit," accessed January 23, 2020, available in Italian and Polish at Vatican.va, par. 4.

"…most defenceless of human beings?"

> John Paul II, *Evangelium Vitae*, par. 70.

16. Care for the Elderly

"… have no choice but to submit."

> John Paul II, *Evangelium Vitae*, par. 19.

"… in his plan of salvation."

> John Paul II, "Letter to the Elderly," accessed January 23, 2020, Vatican.va, pars. 1, 9, 13.

"… also that of others."

> John Paul II, "Letter to the President of the Second World Assembly on Ageing, Madrid," accessed January 23, 2020, Vatican.va.

15. "Saint Maker"

… previous 500 years combined.

> "About Saint John Paul II," Saint John Paul II National Shrine website, accessed January 23, 2020, https://www.jp2shrine.org/en/about/jp2bio.html.

… and beatified 1,341 men and women.

> Francis X. Rocca, "How the Catholic Church Chooses a Saint," *Wall Street Journal*, December 18, 2015, https://www.wsj.com/articles/how-the-catholic-church-chooses-a-saint-1450477239.

"… the example of heroic virtue."

> Weigel, *Witness to Hope*, 221–22.

"… called to holiness and to mission."

> John Paul II, *Redemptoris Missio*, accessed January 23, 2020, Vatican.va, par. 90.

"… let yourselves be won by him!"

> John Paul II, "Homily at Mass at 'Monte del Gozo,' Santiago de Compostela," accessed January 23, 2020, Vatican.va, pars. 6, 8.

14. The Splendor of Truth

"Non datur libertas sine veritate"

> Andrew Nicholas Woznicki, *The Dignity of Man as a Person: Essays on the Christian Humanism of His Holiness John Paul II* (San Francisco: Society of Christ, 1987), 57.

"… in service to human freedom."

> Weigel, *Witness to Hope*, 264.

"… fullness of truth about themselves."

> John Paul II, *Fides et Ratio*, accessed January 23, 2020, Vatican.va, introduction.

"… or together they perish in misery."

> Ibid., par. 90.

"'… Way, the Truth and the Life.'"

> John Paul II, "Address at Longchamp Racecourse," accessed January 23, 2020, Vatican.va, par. 9.

13. Revised Code of Canon Law

"… 1,752 laws and their various subsections."

> Weigel, *Witness to Hope*, 445.

… was Vatican II's final document.

> John Paul II, "Address to the Course Participants on the New Code of Canon Law," accessed January 23, 2020, available in Italian and Portuguese at Vatican.va, par. 2.

"… may be adequately organized."

> John Paul II, *Sacrae Disciplinae Leges*, accessed January 23, 2020, Vatican.va.

12. World Travel

"... all but sixteen of Rome's 336 parishes."

> Weigel, *The End and the Beginning*, 434.

"... born after the visit are named John Paul ..."

> Filip Mazurczak, "How Saint John Paul II Changed the Church and the World," *Catholic World Report*, October 22, 2016, https://www.catholicworldreport.com/2016/10/22/how-st-john-paul-ii-changed-the-church-and-the-world/.

"... to make everyone else tired."

> John Paul II, quoted in "Book Retells Beginning of Press Conferences with John Paul II on Papal Airplane," *Rome Reports in English*, April 20, 2011, https://www.youtube.com/watch?v=8xwnBhri_F0.

"... something of what is too much!"

> Bill Blakemore, "Beatification of John Paul II: Pope Would Give Candid Interviews — at 35,000 Feet," *ABC News*, April 30, 2011, https://abcnews.go.com/International/beatification-john-paul-ii-pope-give-candid-interviews/story?id=13493166.

11. Devotion to the Eucharist

"... manner by every community"

> John Paul II, *Mane Nobiscum Domine*, accessed January 23, 2020, Vatican.va, par. 17.

"... the foundation of the spiritual life"

> John Paul II, "Message to the Seminarians of Spain," accessed January 23, 2020, available in Spanish at Vatican.va, par. 3.

"... from the eucharistic mystery"

> John Paul II, *Ecclesia de Eucharistia*, accessed January 23, 2020, Vatican.va, par. 60.

10. Devotion to Mary

"… the humble Handmaid of Nazareth"

> John Paul II, "Address to the Participants of the 8th Mariological Colloquium," accessed January 23, 2020, Vatican.va, par. 1.

… (Dogmatic Constitution on the Church).

> Weigel, *Witness to Hope*, 162.

"… role in the work of salvation"

> John Paul II, *Redemptoris Mater*, accessed January 23, 2020, Vatican.va, par. 30.

"… Mother of the Church as well."

> John Paul II, "Homily at the Cathedral of Saint Matthew, Washington, DC," accessed January 23, 2020, Vatican.va.

9. Unpacking Vatican II

"… the Church in the Modern World."

> Weigel, *The End and the Beginning*, 67.

"… to secure the legacy of Vatican II."

> Weigel, *Witness to Hope*, 244.

"… evangelizing mission with fresh enthusiasm."

> John Paul II, *Novo Millennio Ineunte*, par. 2.

"… God's Revelation in Jesus Christ."

> John Paul II, "Address to the Conference Studying the Implementation of the Second Vatican Council," accessed January 23, 2020, Vatican.va, par. 4.

"… resources of mind, heart and spirit."

> Sabrina Arena Ferrisi, "John Paul II Meets Vatican II," *Legatus* magazine, May 1, 2010, https://legatus.org /john-paul-ii-meets-vatican-ii/.

"… yesterday, today and for ever!"

> John Paul II, "Address to the Conference Studying the Implementation of the Second Vatican Council," par. 9.

8. Culture of Life

"… heart of the culture of life."
>John Paul II, *Centesimus Annus*, par. 39.

"… the natural point of death."
>John Paul II, "Homily at the Cherry Creek State Park of Denver," accessed January 23, 2020, Vatican.va, par. 3.

"… because it consists in sharing the very life of God"
>John Paul II, *Evangelium Vitae*, par. 2.

"… and in his relations with others."
>Ibid., pars. 95, 48.

"… have no choice but to submit."
>Ibid., par. 19.

7. World Youth Day

… is celebrated in the dioceses.
>Weigel, *Witness to Hope*, 493, 750.

"… preach it from the rooftops!"
>John Paul II, "Homily at the Cherry Creek State Park of Denver," par. 6.

"… to the Church's sacramental life."
>Weigel, *Witness to Hope*, 684.

6. Luminous Mysteries of the Rosary

"… the dreadful scourge of terrorism."
>*L'Osservatore Romano*, October 3, 2001, p. 2.

"… confidently take up the Rosary once again."
>John Paul II, *Rosarium Virginis Mariae*, accessed January 23, 2020, Vatican.va, par. 43.

"… until we attain true holiness."
>Ibid., pars. 1, 26.

… first publishing them in 1973.
>John Formosa and Anthony Cilia, "George Preca and the New Mysteries of the Rosary," Order of Carmelites, accessed January 23, 2020, https://ocarm.org/en/content/ocarm/george-preca-and-new-mysteries-rosary.

"... the definitive revelation of God."

>John Paul II, *Rosarium Virginis Mariae*, par. 19.

"... continuing to use the Rosary."

>Ibid., par. 41.

5. The *Catechism of the Catholic Church*

... for the Eastern Catholic Churches.

>Ralph McInerny, "An Extraordinary Synod," *Crisis*, January 1, 1986, https://www.crisismagazine.com/1986/an-extraordinary-synod-2.

"... fathers, doctors, and saints of the Church."

>Michael J. Wrenn and Kenneth D. Whitehead, "The Importance of the Catechism," *Crisis*, June 1, 1995, https://www.crisismagazine.com/1995/the-importance-of-the-catechism.

"... this would not have been accomplished."

>John Paul II, *Crossing the Threshold of Hope*, 164.

"... coherent, comprehensive, and accessible way."

>Weigel, *Witness to Hope*, 505.

4. The Fall of Communism

"... they also pursued highly positive ideals"

>John Paul II, *Memory and Identity*, 45.

... willing to speak out against evil.

>Kengor, *A Pope and a President*, 192–93.

"... are even now being written."

>Ronald Reagan, Address at University of Notre Dame, May 17, 1981, UVA Miller Center, https://millercenter.org/the-presidency/presidential-speeches/may-17-1981-address-university-notre-dame.

"... individuals and communities have."

>John Paul II, *Redemptor Hominis*, accessed January 23, 2020, Vatican.va, par. 17.

3. Theology of the Body

"… in the unity of that image."

> John Paul II, "General Audience, January 2, 1980," accessed January 23, 2020, Vatican.va.

"… openness to the generation of new life."

> Avery Dulles, "The Theologian," *America*, April 18, 2005, https://www.americamagazine.org/issue/527 /article/theologian.

"… 'out of reverence for Christ.'"

> John Paul II, "General Audience, August 25, 1982," accessed January 23, 2020, Vatican.va, par. 4.

"… in the third millennium of the Church."

> Weigel, *Witness to Hope*, 343.

2. Divine Mercy

"… when he began *Dives in Misericordia*."

> Weigel, *Witness to Hope*, 387.

"… as my task before God."

> John Paul II, "Angelus, November 22, 1981," Vatican.va, par. 2. Available in English at "His 'Personal Task Before God,'" The Divine Mercy, January 18, 2011, accessed December 5, 2019, https://www.thedivinemercy .org/articles/his-personal-task-god.

"… refuge and the light of hope?"

> John Paul II, "Homily at the Beatification of Three Priests and Two Religious Sisters, April 18, 1993," Vatican.va, par. 6. Available in English at "April 18, 1993: Divine Mercy Sunday," The Divine Mercy, https:// www.thedivinemercy.org/message/john-paul-ii /homilies/1993-04-18.

"… a regenerating experience of mercy."

> John Paul II, "Regina Coeli, April 10, 1994," Vatican. va, par. 2. Available in English at "Divine Mercy: A Personal Encounter with Our Savior Himself," The Divine Mercy, https://www.thedivinemercy.org/articles

/divine-mercy-personal-encounter-our-savior-himself.
"… will be called 'Divine Mercy Sunday.'"
>John Paul II, "Homily for the Canonization of Sr. Mary
>Faustina Kowalska," accessed January 23, 2020,
>Vatican.va, par. 4.

"… know ever better the true face of God."
>Ibid., pars. 2, 5.

1. The New Evangelization

"… Christ's sacrifice in the Mass."
>Paul VI, *Evangelii Nuntiandi*, accessed January 23, 2020,
>Vatican.va, par. 14.

"… its ardor, methods and expression."
>John Paul II, "Address to the CELAM Assembly, Port-
>au-Prince, Haiti," Vatican.va, par. 4 (III). English trans-
>lation available at "Disciples Called to Witness: Part
>II," United States Conference of Catholic Bishops,
>accessed January 23, 2020, http://www.usccb.org/be-
>liefs-and-teachings/how-we-teach
>/new-evangelization/disciples-called-to-witness
>/disciples-called-to-witness-part-ii.cfm.

"…which continually calls for a re-evangelization."
>John Paul II, *Christifideles Laici*, accessed January 23,
>2020, Vatican.va, par. 4.

"… a 'new evangelization' or a 're-evangelization.'"
>*John Paul II, Redemptoris Missio, par. 33.*

"… to proclaim Christ to all peoples."
>Ibid., par. 3.

About the Author

PATRICK NOVECOSKY is one of America's most accomplished Catholic communicators. The winner of more than two dozen awards from the Catholic Press Association, he has edited and written for some of America's top Catholic publications and has been published in five languages. Patrick is managing partner at NovaMedia, a public relations firm specializing in the Catholic space. He previously served as *Legatus* magazine's editor-in-chief for twelve years. He's traveled to twenty-six countries, met Pope Saint John Paul II five times, and made Pope Francis laugh out loud. Most importantly, he is a husband and the father of five beautiful children.